EDINBURGH : The Silent City

WALKING THROUGH EDINBURGH WITH STUART MONTGOMERY

ISBN: 978-1-9999251-1-6

Produced by MD Print & Design, Edinburgh
enquiries@mdpd.co.uk

INTRODUCTION

In 2020, the coronavirus pandemic affected the lives of virtually every citizen in the world. The outbreak began in China, in December 2019. Six months later, fourteen million people in nearly two hundred countries had been infected, with half a million deaths recorded from the disease. By mid-July, more than forty thousand people had died in the United Kingdom.

From the 23rd of March the British people were instructed to 'close down', to 'Stay at Home' and protect lives. Shops, (except essential food outlets, pharmacies, post offices and some banks), businesses, offices, schools and universities, churches, bars and restaurants, cinemas, concert halls and theatres, gardens and leisure facilities, all closed their doors to the public until further notice. From this date onwards many people would have to work from home.

Economies across the globe went into recession, families were separated and everyone everywhere became isolated. There was anxiety and the fear of: not seeing our families, losing our jobs, losing our freedom, not being able to pay household bills. All of us were trying desperately to stay well. Most importantly, many thousands of people lost loved ones.

None of this was anyone's fault.

In Britain, at the peak of the virus in April and May, we were allowed to take one period of 'essential exercise' out of doors each day. This was for around an hour, and initially for a distance of up to one mile from home.

Positive aspects emerged during this time; new opportunities that could be embarked upon, even in such sad and difficult circumstances. Living in the centre of Edinburgh I was fortunate in being able to take photographs while walking through the city. Every day I appreciated an atmosphere of silence, tranquillity, and deserted streets that were void of traffic and pedestrians. For three months I discovered the astonishing ambience of a capital city in hibernation.

I felt I had been gifted the keys to a beautiful city, and the breath-taking grandeur of my home town felt more vibrant than ever. For years I had dreamt about the scenes you will see in the following pages. In 2020 I was able to fulfil my dream, to share it with you, and to make a record of scenes that had not been possible before. That said, it clearly is to be regretted that this possibility arose from the tragic situation of the pandemic.

Every photograph has a story to tell. The great British artist L.S. Lowry said: "I paint what I see".

I take photographs and write about what I see: the central image, the colour of the sky, specific features and anything that might be of notable interest.

This is not just a book of photographs, nor is it a reference book. Rather, it is a diary of my walks and journeys during the coronavirus pandemic, between March and June 2020. It is the personal account of what I experienced during that time, in pictures and words.

For many years, I have been accustomed to taking my camera with me when leaving the house, on my walks to the shops or nearby gardens and parks along the river. Even when going to and from work I may see something of interest to photograph.

This is a unique selection of scenes which probably, and it is to be hoped, will never be seen again. Prepare to see Edinburgh's city centre, normally bustling throughout the year, silent and deserted, without human life and void of activity. You will see some of my favourite buildings, gardens, statues, and bridges in this book.

I have researched and written a few details about each picture, giving a little information on my favourite architects and buildings. You will also read about some of my boyhood tales in a few amusing anecdotes.

With fizzy drink bottles and chocolate bars, I took my daily walks under blue skies and warm sunshine, carrying my Canon 1200D SLR camera everywhere I went.

I hope that there is something for everyone in this book, whether you are a resident in Edinburgh or a visitor to the City.

Any profit from the sale of this book will go to St. Columba's Hospice in Edinburgh, and I dedicate it to my father, George.

Please enjoy 'Edinburgh: The Silent City'.

Stuart Montgomery

ABOUT THE AUTHOR

STUART MONTGOMERY is a concert pianist and organist, teacher and amateur photographer.

He has lived and worked in the Stockbridge area of Edinburgh all of his life, and has a particular admiration for the buildings designed and built between 1750 and 1850.

Having grown up surrounded by some of the finest architecture in Britain it is perhaps not surprising to learn that when Stuart travels out of Scotland's Capital, on holiday or for work, he says 'the best thing about leaving Edinburgh is the thought of coming back to it again'.

ST COLUMBA'S HOSPICE CARE

Thank you for supporting St Columba's Hospice Care by purchasing this book.

St Columba's exists to give everyone who needs it the very best Hospice Care. We are an independent charity at the heart of our local community, offering flexible and person-centred services to our patients and families. Our specialist support is available free of charge to those who need it most, wherever they are in our community.

In 2020, we began adapting our services to provide care in new and inclusive ways - be that at home, in care settings or at the Hospice. We have delivered these with the compassion and quality you know.

Our dedicated staff now offer a range of care to our patients and their families at our Hospice building, at our outreach clinics in East Lothian and in the community across Edinburgh and the Lothians, from Queensferry to Dunbar.

Our new Access Team offers expert advice to patients, families and health professionals at first point of contact and helps them access the right service at the right time. Our new Hospice at Home service provides practical, social and emotional support to our patients and their carers, enabling and empowering them at home. We are adapting our supportive care services too, with new resources available by phone and online to help families and patients through difficult times.

As well as providing care, the Hospice is committed to education, research, collaborative projects and community initiatives, helping our Hospice and other care providers deliver the very best support to vulnerable people.

St Columba's Hospice is a registered charity and most of the funds needed are generated through fundraising. 82p of every £1 is spent directly on patient care with the other 18p going towards raising the next £1. So, the generosity of our community of supporters directly helps us to maintain our invaluable services for the people of Edinburgh and the Lothians.

In aid of St Columba's Hospice Care

ACKNOWLEDGEMENTS

I never imagined I would be able to create a book of my photographs and stories, and especially during the difficult times we endured in 2020.

Much of the belief in myself to do this was due to the support and encouragement from my family, and many friends and associates, all of whom I would like to thank for helping me to achieve this publication.

All the photographs in this book and the accompanying stories are the property and copyright of Stuart Montgomery, taken between March and June 2020.

I would like to acknowledge: 'The Buildings of Scotland (Edinburgh)', by John Gifford, Colin McWilliam and David Walker (1984). This book is inspiring with much to learn; and what great pleasure I subsequently gained by going out to study and photograph so many streets and buildings in and around the City.

My sincere thanks to Dr Neil Price for his encouragement, and for pointing me in the right direction of MD Print and Design. Sandra and Dave Lennie have been marvellous at each stage of production in supporting all I aspired to achieve.

My mother, Nancy, was cared for in her last weeks during November 1994 at St. Columba's Hospice in Edinburgh. For that, I am happy to give a share of the proceeds from this publication to the Hospice. I would like to say thank-you to Diane Ewart and the Hospice team for their help.

Throughout the period of preparation and production I felt totally supported by my dear mentors and editors Dr. Charles Anderson, of the University of Edinburgh and Mr. Frank Mitchell, of The Scottish Tramway and Transport Society. Special thanks to you both.

And to my wonderful dad, George, for all your encouragement and help as always, at this time and throughout my life with everything I have tried to do. I dedicate my book to you, in your honour.

A SILENT QUEEN STREET

For three months, between March and June 2020, scenes like this became the norm and an ambience of tranquillity and calm settled across Edinburgh.

In this new silent city, the air was cleaner, we enjoyed our 'local' walks meandering through deserted streets, and we admired buildings and gardens as though the city had been opened just for us.

Here on Queen Street I listened to the bird song. I saw bees that were bigger than usual. There was no traffic to speak of, and a golden hush that I wished might go on for ever.

This photograph was taken mid-afternoon on a Wednesday in April.

THE BELL TOWER

This is a scene I have tried to capture on camera for years and what joy it was to be able to get it at last. It is virtually impossible, during daylight hours, to photograph the Bell Tower clock on Lothian Road without pedestrians passing by.

The clock was presented to the City of Edinburgh by Arthur Bell & Sons, Scotch whisky distillers of Perth, in 1962. Until quite recently it was situated on the other side of Lothian Road at the bus stop in front of the Usher Hall. It has a soprano-like Westminster chime which strikes every fifteen minutes. It is alleged that the clock was moved owing to audiences in the Usher Hall claiming they could hear the chiming over the music! The chimes were rather eccentric in rhythm but highly amusing to hear, nicely piercing too, but the clock hasn't chimed since 2002.

When the chimes functioned, on evenings when I went to the Usher Hall for a concert commencing at 7.30, I always tried to be there a little before 7 in order to hear it chiming on the hour.

THE USHER HALL

Edinburgh's most famous concert venue, the Usher Hall has hosted concerts and events since its construction in 1914. It can hold nearly three thousand people in its recently restored auditorium and is well loved by performers all over the world. Everyone adores its fabulous acoustics.

The construction of the hall was funded by Andrew Usher, the son of a whisky distiller, and the final cost was one hundred and thirty-four thousand pounds. Sadly, Mr. Usher died before building work was even started.

I remember being taken here as a little boy in the 1970s to see world renowned pianists perform concertos with famous orchestras, notably Arthur Rubinstein, Claudio Arrau, and Moura Lympany. I also heard the singers Janet Baker, Joan Sutherland and countless others. Later, it was great fun in 1997 going to see Tony Blair give one of his election speeches and hearing D:Ream perform that brilliant song 'Things can only get better'. I loved that.

Today, the Usher Hall is the Edinburgh venue for the Royal Scottish National Orchestra; and, oh yes I've performed here in concerts myself now and again, notably for the launch of Alexander McCall Smith's novel '44 Scotland Street'.

ROBERT ADAM'S GENERAL REGISTER HOUSE

How wonderfully grand this building must have looked when new.

General Register House, with its little clock tower seen on the right, is arguably the finest Georgian building in Edinburgh. Its principal architect was Robert Adam. Construction of this magnificent building, to be used for the retention of public records, was completed in 1786 and it is the only one of Adam's public buildings in Edinburgh that he saw complete.

The statue of the man on the black horse is the Duke of Wellington, created later by Sir John Steell.

This photograph was taken on a Monday afternoon in April 2020.

CALTON ROAD AND REGENT BRIDGE

Regent Bridge is situated on Waterloo Place, above the street that leads to the back of Waverley Station. Construction began in 1816, under the supervision of Robert Stevenson, and the bridge was completed four years later in a neo-classical style with a semi-circular arch, forty-five feet in height.

The principal arch is ornamented by two open arches supported by Corinthian columns, and these are more easily visible from Waterloo Place.

GEORGE IV

The statue of George IV stands at the summit of Hanover Street and George Street. It looks south, almost into the eyes of the young Queen Victoria, who sits on top of the RSA in Princes Street. George IV lived and reigned at the time of the building of what is known today as the Georgian 'New Town'.

The bronze statue, constructed in 1831 by Sir Francis Chantrey, commemorates the King's visit to Edinburgh in 1822. I stood in the middle of the road in Hanover Street, an impossible position to be in normally, to capture this photograph without traffic or people anywhere to be seen. This was at 2.30 on a Thursday afternoon in April 2020.

GEORGE IV.
VISITED
SCOTLAND
MDCCCXXII.

THE ROYAL SCOTTISH ACADEMY OF ART

Edinburgh's Royal Scottish Academy, late Georgian architecture at its most beautiful, is William Henry Playfair's masterpiece of the 1830s.

Playfair was one of Scotland's leading architects of his time, and his two classical art temples on the Mound sit together in joyous harmony on Princes Street against the towering backdrop of Edinburgh Castle.

Observe the fluted Doric ashlar columns of Craigleith sandstone and these corner pediments, features characteristic of Classical Edinburgh.

In 1837 the Royal Institution for the Encouragement of the Fine Arts commissioned the sculptor Sir John Steell to carve eight sphinxes which are positioned on top of the building, and some are visible in these photographs.

High up, overseeing everything beneath sits this statue of the young Queen Victoria with crown and sceptre, also created by Steell; her robes draped to portray her as Britannia. Unveiled in 1844, this statue was initially intended for Buckingham Palace in London but it came to Edinburgh instead.

HENDERSONS

Hendersons was one of the best known and loved vegetarian restaurants in Scotland and for fifty-eight years it enjoyed an international reputation.

It opened in 1962; and if you live in the Capital, or if you've visited Edinburgh during the Festival or any other time of the year, then you will know this famous place on Hanover Street.

Hendersons went into voluntary liquidation at the start of July 2020, and this is one of hundreds of hospitality businesses that have closed their doors permanently owing to the coronavirus pandemic.

Hendersons offered a mouth-watering range of vegetarian and vegan cuisine, serving food using fresh and local products. It was one of the most perfect places to dine and very much part of the cultural fabric of Edinburgh. You could hear live music on most nights, and throughout its history the management was always happy to host performers of all styles.

ST. BERNARD'S CRESCENT

St. Bernard's Crescent and its surrounding streets belong to James Milne's architectural design of the 1820s. Its central feature is these magnificent Doric columns.

The Charlotte Lanterns, emulating the lamps of the period of its construction, are relatively new and bring an added note of elegance to what is one of my favourite crescents. There are several examples of these light fittings elsewhere on the following pages.

RAMSAY GARDEN

The houses in the foreground on Ramsay Garden are handsome Scottish vernacular buildings and one of the most outstanding things about living here is the view!

Developed in the 1890s by urban planner Patrick Geddes, Ramsay Garden started out as Ramsay Lodge, an octagonal house designed by, and for, the poet and wig-maker Allan Ramsay, in the 1730s.

This is the courtyard which is clearly loved and cared for. Note the pointed stonework with decorative painted window surrounds, and these russet staircases with their attractive iron hand-rails.

I like the deep pediment of the building at the far end and one can sense the pride that those who dwell here take in for their surroundings.

ST. JOHN'S HIGHLAND TOLBOOTH KIRK

On a Monday afternoon in April I was struck by the dramatic emptiness of this scene. Where is everybody? I felt my body freeze and stood here for some ten minutes. Silence, calm, nothing. Stare down this path and feel the eerie calm. Behold, Edinburgh, the silent city.

The most distinguished building in the photograph is the former St. John's Highland Tolbooth Kirk, a fine example of Gothic Revival architecture, designed by James Gillespie Graham and Augustus Pugin. Constructed between 1842 and 1845, it was originally designed as a meeting hall for the General Assembly of the Church of Scotland.

From 1929, the building was used as a church until the mid-1980s and today it is the home of the Edinburgh International Festival 'Hub', used as a ticket office and performance venue.

PRINCES STREET GARDENS

East Princes Street Gardens in springtime, and how pleasant it is to see these circular flower beds framed against a cluster of dark clouds.

The crude advancement of commercial progress has dictated this haven of tranquillity be transformed at Christmas time and during the Edinburgh International Festival each August into an ever expanding market place. The revenue gained to the city is considerable, but look at this scene with its flower beds and quiet beauty.

During the coronavirus pandemic we learned to live differently, and there was time to stop and stare, and time to appreciate the finer things around us. Instead of having a commercial market and fun-fair here let's try and preserve the ambience of this and other similar green spaces, as more of a priority than we may have done before. 2020 slowed us down and it's time for us to rethink the way we would like to live.

The statue of Edinburgh's Lord Provost and Member of Parliament Adam Black, who lived until 1874, is one of many in Princes Street Gardens.

CHARLOTTE SQUARE AND PRINCE ALBERT

Charlotte Square mirrors St. Andrew Square in the east, and is today designated a World Heritage Site. Initially named St. George's Square in James Craig's original plan, it was renamed in 1786 and was the last part of the first phase of Edinburgh's New Town, completed around 1820. Much of it was formed to the 1791 design of Robert Adam, who died one year later just as building work began.

James Gillespie Graham, James Milne, Robert Matheson, David Bryce, William Burn, William Henry Playfair, Robert Reid, Thomas Hamilton and Robert Adam are just a few of the design heroes of that period.

The square comprises many architectural delights including: central Greek pediments, Doric columns and rustic stonework on the ground floors, arched stone entrances with mouchette fanlights, all of which contribute to the power, grandeur and unified design of the square. Note how it is flanked by these ornate Charlotte lanterns.

The central garden was originally laid out by William Weir in 1808. In 1861

a plan was drawn up by Robert Matheson, Clerk of Works for Scotland, for a larger and more square garden centred upon a memorial to the newly deceased Prince Albert, consort of Queen Victoria. The bronze statue of Albert, in the uniform of a Field Marshal, is surrounded by four figures depicting 'Nobility', 'Army and Navy', 'Labour', and 'Science and Learning'. It was created by Sir John Steell in 1876; the base of the statue and the figures are by different artists.

The original intention was that the statue would sit in the centre of the eastern edge of the garden, facing along George Street. The central open space is a private garden, available to owners of the surrounding properties, and during the month of August each year the garden plays host to the Edinburgh International Book Festival.

The railings around the garden were removed in 1940 as part of the war effort and the current railings date from 1947.

MEMORIAL TO THE ROYAL SCOTS GREYS

With the fragrance and colour of spring all around, here sits Major Anthony James Hinnigan, from Jedburgh, on his horse Polly.

This bronze memorial was created by William Birnie Rhind and unveiled in 1906 to commemorate the Royal Scots Greys, a cavalry regiment of the British Army who fought in the second Boer War.

The regiment was formed in 1678, and amalgamated with the 3rd Carabiniers and the Royal Scots Dragoon Guards in 1971.

THE ROSS FOUNTAIN

How great it is to see the Ross Fountain in West Princes Street Gardens restored and operating again. On the continent there are fountains in many cities, but sadly there are so few in Scotland.

The cast iron fountain was made in France and was exhibited at the 1862 Great Exhibition where it was purchased by gunmaker Daniel Ross, gifted to the city of Edinburgh and installed in 1872.

In 2008 the water was turned off. Restoration began in 2017 by 'Lost Art Limited of Wigan', on behalf of The Ross Development Trust, at a cost of nearly two million pounds.

In July 2018, the fountain was functioning again, restored to its original splendour, and newly painted in turquoise, brown and gold.

EDINBURGH'S WEST END

I have always wanted to take this photograph, void of traffic and pedestrians.

Here are three magnificent buildings to admire: Edinburgh Castle watching over everything below; St. Cuthbert's Church with its ancient graveyard; but let's focus on the building in the centre, St. John's Church.

St. John's Church, on the corner of Lothian Road and Princes Street, is Episcopalian and throughout the 19th century became a fashionable place of worship for some of the more wealthy residents of the developing New Town.

It was designed in 1816 by William Burn and as can be seen the architecture is exquisite, as is the interior decoration.

Today, and for several recent decades, St. John's has been an important location for world political causes, for campaigns to assist the poorer areas of the globe.

During the coronavirus pandemic Lothian Buses operated a skeleton service for more than three months, and here comes one of our seventy seven fleet of Volvo / Alexander Dennis Limited Enviro 400s — vehicles which can transport up to one hundred and twenty nine people. This is the star bus of the fleet in Lothian's Centenary livery.

I stood here for some ten minutes in the refreshing and clean air, simply to admire all that there is to see in this scene. It really was inspiring.

ST. STEPHEN'S CHURCH

On the clock, the time is just after five minutes to three.

Walk down the steep hill from Frederick Street and Howe Street, northwards towards Stockbridge and your eyes will meet with this architectural hymn of praise dominating the Edinburgh skyline. Rising up from the foot of the hill it is a masterpiece of design.

St. Stephen's Church was completed in 1828 and designed by William Henry Playfair - my favourite architect, and oh to have met that man!

The church also houses one of the finest pipe organs in Scotland — a Father Willis in virtually its original condition from 1881. It is a fabulous instrument and one I have had the pleasure of playing several times.

Note also the glorious stonework on this corner block, with all the fine features of the early 1800s. It is on Great King Street, designed by Robert Reid.

It was nice to be able to hear the clock chiming a few minutes after I took this photograph.

'MR. MONTY'S' TRUMPTON CLOCK

Once upon a time, when I was very little, my mum would bring me down the hill to the shops here and say: 'What's the time on the clock?' I'd then say, "It's ten to eleven and that's the Trumpton clock."

People of a certain generation may remember the three television series of programmes for younger viewers called Camberwick Green, Trumpton and Chigley, created by Gordon Murray and narrated by Brian Cant. These were adorable fifteen minute miniatures which are still available to buy and I love to curl up on the settee with a bowl of popcorn and watch a few episodes. There are thirteen for each series.

At the start of the Trumpton programmes we see a large clock in the square and it looks similar to this one — maybe that's why I developed my love for clocks.

On this glorious day in April I could hardly believe my luck. A pure blue sky, the sun was in the right place, and no traffic or pedestrians.

We're in the heart of Stockbridge beside the bridge over the Water of Leith, and this charming building makes me pause every time I pass by. It was built in 1900 by McGibbon and Ross and was once a former Edinburgh Savings Bank, but today it is home to an Italian restaurant.

This was one of those occasions, when I captured the photo I wanted to rush home and show everyone. My mum would have been pleased!

SAXE COBURG PLACE GARDENS

Tucked away behind Stockbridge on a raised plateau is Saxe Coburg Place with its central garden, one of the more desirable addresses in Edinburgh.

The building design is from the office of James Milne in the early 1820s and a deep U-shaped crescent was planned, but due to a lack of finance to complete the project it was never finished, leaving a gap at the far end. This has remained ever since, and a staircase named by locals the 'Snakey' provides a handy shortcut to the Colonies and Raeburn Place in Stockbridge.

And then in 1897 along came Glenogle swimming pool, which can be entered from Saxe Coburg Place.

In the centre is this garden oasis of calm with Stockbridge Church (formerly St.

Bernard's Church) in the distance and here, in the springtime, all of nature enjoys its young and vibrant bloom.

Stare at these scenes for long enough and your mind will be transported into a more peaceful place, and how pleasant it must be to look out of these drawing room windows. Imagine yourself sitting on that bench, enjoying the warm sunshine and the peace of the garden.

During the coronavirus pandemic I discovered many things about myself, including a renewed engagement with art, music, gardens and architecture.

Appreciation of the finer arts can bring us a new sense of meaning, with more time to reflect, and perhaps a more gentle, inner contentment.

HENDERSON ROW

In the 1820s local architect James Milne was highly active in providing plans and drawings for streets and buildings in the New Town, and two hundred years later these buildings are still standing proudly.

We're on the corner of Henderson Row and Dundas Street, where I live. Edinburgh was perhaps lucky not to be bombed in wartime as severely as other cities, and all around the centre of the Capital there is stonework to be admired of the sort you are looking at here, including the decorative rustic ashlar around the doors of the corner pavilioned block.

Note the little pediments above the first floor windows and over to the left, that delicious portico at number 6 with its Ionic columns — several houses in the street have these. The first floor apartment with the net curtains was once owned by the late Mrs. Joan Scott, a grand Edinburgh lady.

Henderson Row is fascinating for its former industries and public buildings: historic mills, a wash house, the former Edinburgh Northern Cable Tramways depot (designed by William Hamilton Beattie of Jenners and the Balmoral Hotel), and Edinburgh Academy School which doubles as the 'Marcia Blaine School' in the film of The Prime of Miss Jean Brodie, with Maggie Smith and Gordon Jackson.

Originally, these basements were shops and, in accordance with normal procedure at the time, streets with the name of 'Row' would nearly always have been built on one side only, with gardens opposite them.

THE SHORE

The Water of Leith started its flow in the Pentland Hills and is almost at its journey's end. It will end at the mouth of the sea a few hundred yards further on.

The Shore is a vibrant hub of life with some famous restaurants and a lively selection of pubs. Normally it would be buzzing with activity, especially on a sunny day like this.

This part of the river is a popular location for swans to build their nests and rear their young. Residents and walkers can observe the cygnets growing from week to week during the spring and summer months. Two nests can be seen here and each may have up to six or seven cygnets.

My dad and I like to walk along the old railway line between Scotland Street and the Shore, and we often visit the little Café Truva, (out of shot to the right), to enjoy a cup of tea or coffee, with some of their delicious home-made shortbread.

The steamer boat is called Ocean Mist. It was constructed during the First World War, one of around five hundred vessels built to replace fishing trawlers, many of which were lost to enemy action. Ocean Mist is the only one that survives today. The boat has been a floating restaurant, and in 2020 it is undergoing renovation.

THE PLAYHOUSE

Once upon a time Edinburgh had some forty picture houses, but perhaps the most famous was the Playhouse, notably for the visit of Stan Laurel and Oliver Hardy, and also for its glorious organ that would rise up from the basement to entertain audiences.

The Playhouse, built by John Fairweather of Glasgow in 1927/29, is the largest theatre in the United Kingdom and for ninety years this building has served a dual purpose as cinema-cum-theatre. The auditorium was designed to hold over three thousand people.

I was moved to see the Playhouse like this. Never in recent decades has it been possible to capture a photograph during the daytime, with the whole scene void of traffic or people.

THE VUE, LEITH STREET

Edinburgh has gained several impressive and award-winning modern buildings in recent decades, but sometimes they don't always sit comfortably alongside their older, architectural sisters and brothers.

There are several awkward juxtapositions of new and old buildings in my view, but that doesn't apply to the VUE cinema complex on Leith Street. Much controversy surrounded this site in the past, an area demolished in the 1960s. Our City Fathers had grand plans for an opera house, then for the headquarters of BBC Scotland, but all these plans were scrapped and in 2002 when we were given this complex.

This is a giant cinema complex of twelve screens, some in digital 3D with all the latest in mesmerizing vision and surround sound. We may need new eyes and ears if technology progresses any further!

I like glass facades, particularly the stylish curvature here, taking the eye all the way along the front and aligning with the Playhouse at the far end. There's a nice big airy feel about this building with plenty of room around the edges, unlike some others that appear to be squeezed into a space made for a much smaller building.

The giraffe sculptures are apt for the modern day, in the same way perhaps as the Duke of Wellington's statue on horseback, in front of General Register House at the east end of Princes Street, would have been in the mid-19th century.

BALMORAL (NORTH BRITISH) HOTEL

The Balmoral opened in 1902 as the North British Hotel, a traditional railway hotel adjacent to Waverley Station, located at number 1 Princes Street.

The majestic clock tower, (fifty-eight metres in height), is an Edinburgh landmark which can be seen from all around the city centre and beyond. Given that the hotel is adjacent to the station, the clock has enjoyed the tradition of being set two to three minutes fast to ensure that people don't miss their trains, except on New Year's Eve of course!

This ravishing, grandly romantic structure, lavishly endowed with sumptuous ornamentation, formed part of the new North Bridge, following demolition of the Georgian building on the same site — a more modest building, and classical in proportion.

In 1895 William Hamilton Beattie submitted the design for a competition and it won. He had also been working on the new Jenners department store which opened in that year. The NB, (as it will always be known to many older town residents and railway enthusiasts), is the Edinburgh icon seen on television news programmes.

It is such a powerful landmark, strong and dominating; but I wonder how Edinburgh would have viewed this at the start of the 20th century, especially as Princes Street was then largely composed of classically designed buildings where the accent was on ordered symmetry.

It is twenty-five minutes past six on the clock and time to go home for tea. On the sixth week of lockdown restrictions, Edinburgh was clearly sticking to the rules of 'Stay at Home'.

THE ROSS BANDSTAND

The Ross Bandstand in the centre of West Princes Street Gardens, dating from 1935, is named after William Henry Ross, Chairman of the Distillers Company. He donated eight thousand pounds to the cost of the present building and terraces; and many a fine performance can be enjoyed from the open-air pop-up seating arena in the foreground. The 1935 bandstand replaced a cast-iron, circular Victorian structure.

Every August, during the Edinburgh International Festival, the world famous fireworks display takes place from the Castle above, with a live concert given by the Scottish Chamber Orchestra. This is also the central venue for Edinburgh's annual Hogmanay concert.

Over to the left we can see the former Highland Tolbooth Kirk, the highest steeple in Edinburgh, with Ramsay Garden below.

DONALDSON'S SCHOOL

I hadn't studied the former Donaldson's School A-listed building before and was delighted to discover its architect was the great William Henry Playfair. It's built around a quadrangle in a kind of Tudor style with large corner towers. Queen Victoria opened it in 1850, (though it wasn't completed until a year later), and apparently she said it was more impressive than many of her palaces!

The building of Donaldson's School was funded by Sir James Donaldson, a publisher who died in 1830. The original plan was to accommodate two hundred pupils, allowing for special bursaries for poor children. Not all were deaf, although applications on behalf of deaf children were encouraged. From 1938, pupils were exclusively deaf.

After more than one hundred and fifty years Donaldson's Trust decided that the building was no longer fit for purpose and they couldn't afford to maintain it. In 2003 it was put up for sale and purchased by property developer Cala Homes, for twenty-two million pounds. The school continued to use the building until 2008 when work commenced on converting the whole site into luxury flats. This was completed in 2015.

ST. BERNARD'S WELL

Stroll along the Water of Leith between Stockbridge and the Dean Village and you will pass St. Bernard's Well, originally built as a small well-house in 1760 in the Dean Valley.

The waters of the well were held in high repute for their medicinal qualities, and the nobility and gentry would visit the valley to drink the water and take in the country air along the Water of Leith.

Built by John Wilson in 1789, this circular Greek temple is supported by ten Doric columns. Observe the centre-piece statue of Hygieia the Greek goddess of health which was made in 1791 from Coade stone (named after Eleanor Coade, one of the world's first recognised women architects).

In the 1940s the well closed to the public, but it was restored in 2013 and is now maintained by the City of Edinburgh Council. It is open again for two hours on occasional Sundays between June and November.

HAYMARKET IN THE RUSH HOUR

At the end of the sixth week of the lockdown restrictions, due to the coronavirus pandemic, we can observe from this picture how Edinburgh was sticking very much to the rules of 'staying at home'.

This photo was taken at 5pm on a weekday afternoon in April, and although there was growing evidence in some cities of more cars and pedestrians, the stillness seen here was very much as it had been in the Capital at the end of March.

You can never plan for everything to go the way you want to when photographing aspects of life, especially when there are moving images that change position, but I was rather taken by this huge bird with its extended wing span flying into the direction of the camera.

EAST PRINCES STREET GARDENS, ALLAN RAMSAY AND THE FLORAL CLOCK

During the coronavirus restrictions the east wing of Princes Street Gardens (top left) was not open to the public, due to ongoing new landscaping of the area. How nice that this has been kept as a walking and seating area of tranquillity, and what a view, taken from Waverley Bridge. Sadly, however, several trees have been removed on the eastern side of the RSA gallery.

The tall spire of the Highland Tolbooth Kirk, (the highest in the Capital), is high up on the left. Sweeping round from it, you can see to the right Ramsay Garden and the Castle. Beneath the Castle is Playfair's magnificent National Gallery constructed in the 1830s.

On the corner of Princes Street and the Mound there is a little haven of tranquillity and charm on the edge of what is normally an area bustling with people and traffic (top right).

The statue is of the poet Allan Ramsay, erected in 1850. First and foremost a poet and writer, Ramsay was born in Lanarkshire in 1688 and it was said at the time that his pleasant manners and varied cultural work, including painting and the overseeing of some architectural developments, contributed to him being a popular figure. He died in 1758.

His first trade was as a wig-maker and in the early 1700s he established himself in Edinburgh's High Street. When I was little I assumed that men around this time grew their hair long and then had it styled and shaped, as we see in the paintings of aristocrats and of musicians, like Bach and Handel. I never realised that actually very few people wore wigs, only the rich and affluent sons of lords and ladies. My mother would wonder why, when we went to stately homes, I would ask her if my hair would grow like that one day!

Gradually, from around 1720, Ramsay was achieving recognition as a writer of songs, sonnets and poetry, and later his work was published in volumes of poetry. His eldest son, also called Allan, was a celebrated portrait painter. In 1846, just after the Scott Monument was built, his name was inscribed, along with other poets, on the lower section of the monument. He is buried in Greyfriars Kirkyard and has a plaque on the south side wall.

Beneath Ramsay's statue is the famous floral garden (bottom right), with thousands of artistically arranged flowers blooming throughout the summer months.

Edinburgh's floral clock (bottom left), at the entrance to West Princes Street Gardens, was the first in the world, made in 1902 for the coronation of King Edward VII. The clock started to tick for the first time on the 10th of June 1903. A year later, city clockmakers James Ritchie and Son installed a cuckoo clock mechanism, just below Ramsay's monument here, but the current cuckoo house wasn't installed until the 1950s. Throughout the summer months, groups of tourists can be seen waiting for the cuckoo to appear, and every fifteen minutes the somewhat large bird comes out to entertain its audience, (but don't be surprised if it's a few minutes late!).

There are no hands on the floral clock in 2020 but in previous years its hands were adorned with every colour of plant, forming a rich tapestry to enchant the passer-by.

As can be seen, the surrounding flower garden is meticulously maintained, and note the rich bed of begonias and many other colourful plants and flowers. In 1974 the floral clock display was especially attractive, in celebration of one hundred years of Princes Street Gardens.

MANSFIELD TRAQUAIR

The Mansfield Traquair Centre is located at the foot of Broughton Street.

A former Catholic Apostolic Church, it was designed by the nineteenth-century architect Sir Robert Rowand Anderson and completed in 1885. It features, as you can see, a beautiful stained glass rose window.

The most outstanding feature of this building is the vast scheme of romantic mural decoration, painted in the 1890s by Scotland's leading Arts and Crafts artist Phoebe Anna Traquair. These murals are considered to be some of the finest in Scotland.

The church suffered badly in the years since it ceased to be a place of worship, and damage to both the fabric of the building and the murals was severe. The Mansfield Traquair Trust was set up in 1993 to preserve this fine building, with a multi-million pound renovation of the building being completed in 2002. The restoration of the murals was completed shortly after.

Mansfield Traquair has been described by some historians as 'Edinburgh's Sistine Chapel'.

I am standing in the middle of the road at this busy junction, where the roundabout is normally constantly occupied by motor vehicles. With the afternoon sunshine just in the right position, what a golden opportunity this was to capture the photograph.

THE ATHENS PARTHENON AND NELSON'S COLUMN

Two of Edinburgh's most iconic structures can be seen here together on Calton Hill. Most striking is the national memorial to the soldiers who died fighting in the Napoleonic Wars in the early 1800s.

It was designed during 1823/26 by Charles Robert Cockerell and William Henry Playfair, and is modelled upon the Parthenon in Athens. Construction started in 1826 but the money ran out! It was then left unfinished, acquiring some rather unfortunate nicknames which have survived to this day: 'Scotland's Folly'; 'Edinburgh's Disgrace'; and 'The Pride and Poverty of Scotland'.

There are twelve towering columns and one can only wonder how magnificent this memorial would have been had it been completed. It must also have been very frustrating for Cockerell and Playfair to see their plans thwarted like this.

On the right is the Nelson column. This is in commemoration of Admiral Lord Nelson's death at the Battle of Trafalgar in 1805. Completed in 1816, the tower is one hundred and six feet high, with one hundred and forty-three steps from the base. As I discovered a few years ago, ascending the staircase is best accomplished by slim people as the spiralling curvature of the steps is steep and narrow. Once you get to the top, there's a viewing platform with some of the best panoramic views of the Capital.

A time ball was installed in 1852 to allow ships in the Forth to know the exact time. On week days it ascends the flagpole and then drops down to signal the firing of Edinburgh Castle's One O' Clock Gun.

I love to stand on Waterloo Place at five to one (Mondays-Fridays) to observe the white ball climbing up the pole, and then....BANG! A unique tradition.

A PLAYFAIR HAVEN

The City Observatory is an astronomical centre on Calton Hill, designed by one of the principal architects of the day William Henry Playfair. Inspired by a Greek temple of the Four Winds, the Observatory was designed in 1818.

Observe the boundary wall and at its corner the magnificent classical monument dedicated to John Playfair, president of the Edinburgh Astronomical Institution.

It can be difficult to capture a photograph here like this, owing to the large number of tourists who visit the hill all the year round.

THE SCOTTISH NATIONAL PORTRAIT GALLERY

The Scottish National Portrait Gallery on Queen Street enjoys the reputation of being unique in Edinburgh's architectural history. There's nothing else in this style in the Capital and what a tempting opportunity it was to snap at this with no traffic or pedestrians — the time was just approaching 6pm on a Wednesday in April.

This powerful, Gothic revival building in red sandstone was paid for by John Ritchie Findlay, main proprietor of The Scotsman newspaper, who masterminded the construction and appointed the architect Sir Robert Rowand Anderson, who also designed Mansfield Traquair (see pages 34 and 35).

Designed in the late 1880s, (within the same decade as Mansfield Traquair), it served both as a museum for the collection of Scottish Antiquities and as the Scottish National Portrait Gallery. It amalgamated with the Royal Scottish Museum (Chambers Street) in 1985 and then closed in 2007 for a comprehensive refurbishment; re-opening in 2009 solely as a portrait gallery in the control of National Galleries of Scotland.

Let's look at it in more detail and observe the pointed arches on those windows, and see how the building is given greater authority by these corner towers.

One can stand here for many minutes, looking up at these turrets which enclose and anchor the building. The sculptures of notable Scots set in to the stonework were designed by William Birnie Rhind, a very busy man in Edinburgh at the time.

In contrast to the disciplined classicism of Playfair, Milne, Burn and others in the 1770/1830 period, this uncompromising Gothic building may have seemed to some Edinburgh citizens in the 1880s a shocking intrusion into the New Town's ordered streets.

ST. MICHAEL'S CHURCH

2020 marks twenty-eight years of my musical directorship at St. Michael's Parish Church on Slateford Road. It has been an honour to work here, to fulfil God's work and to have had three ministers who have inspired everything I have accomplished in church music: Margaret Forrester, James Aitken and Andrea Price.

You won't meet a group of people more warm and caring than those inside that building. It is a unique and totally special place, reflecting the nature of Slateford, Gorgie and Dalry. Services are held every Sunday morning and visitors can expect a warm welcome, with tea and homemade baking at the end of the service.

At the intersection of Slateford Road and Harrison Road, the church was designed by architect John Honeyman and built in 1883. It is A-listed and generally regarded as the best church in the Capital of its style and period. The tower is a prominent and admired landmark all over the city.

One of Lothian Buses' hybrids Volvo B5LH / Wright Gemini 3, number 570 (SA15 VUW) is waiting at the traffic lights on a Service 35. This is the last number of the fleet group from 2015 (group 551-570).

ANN STREET

Built two hundred years ago Ann Street was named by local painter Henry Raeburn after his wife Ann Edgar. Its design was a joint effort between Raeburn and the architect James Milne, who was designing other streets in the area.

Writer, poet and historian Sir John Betjeman said Ann Street is "one of the most attractive in the whole of Britain". The author J.M. Barrie, creator of Peter Pan, based his 1902 novel 'Quality Street' on Ann Street. The Queen Mother, wife of King George VI, visited this street in the early years of her husband's reign.

It's a rare example of a New Town street with private front gardens and all the houses are complete, with no commercial properties and none converted into flats.

WAVERLEY : THE SILENT STATION

No, I didn't arrange for this to happen! It is just after 4.30pm on a weekday afternoon in May, seven weeks after the coronavirus restrictions began. This is an extraordinary scene, where the trains are running on a much reduced service, but few are travelling.

Waverley is Edinburgh's principal railway station, the second busiest station in Scotland after Glasgow Central. It is the northern terminus of the East Coast Main Line, three hundred and ninety-three miles from London King's Cross, although some trains continue to other Scottish destinations beyond Edinburgh.

THE HALFWAY HOUSE

This pub called the Halfway House, on Fleshmarket Close, is up the steps from Market Street opposite the entrance to Waverley Station.

It's one of the more popular pubs in the Old Town and has a wide range of ales and spirits to suit every taste. It's especially appealing for railway travellers arriving in Edinburgh and I often take guests here when they alight from the train.

It has a cosy ambience with traditional, low-timbered ceilings and you always get a warm welcome. The stovies are brilliant and I believe they also do a fine Cullen skink. The title refers to the rest-and-be-thankful stop-over between Market Street and the Royal Mile, such steep terrain even for the fittest.

THE TRON

The High Street — peaceful and in tranquil slumbers.

On this day I felt I was a tourist in my own home town. Throughout the year, hundreds of thousands of visitors meander up and down this ancient street with its whin-sett road surface but on this day it was all mine, just for me. I was a solitary wanderer in the silent city.

The Tron Kirk is one of the great landmarks on the Royal Mile. It was built in the 1600s but closed as a church in 1952.

Having stood empty for over fifty years it was used briefly as a tourist information centre, and today it is the site of the Edinburgh World Heritage Exhibition.

As can be seen on the church clock the time is ten minutes to four on a Thursday afternoon in May. I must prepare to take my leave of this deafening and beautiful silence.

41

ST. GILES CATHEDRAL

Saint Giles, also known as Giles the Hermit, is the patron saint of Edinburgh. He was a Greek Christian hermit saint from Athens and he spent much of his life in Provence, in the south of France.

The Cathedral forms the north side of Parliament Square on Edinburgh's High Street with the law courts on the south side. The building dates from the 14th century onwards and its distinctive crown steeple is one of our best-known landmarks.

St. Giles boasts a wonderful choral tradition and the legendary Herrick Bunney became music master here in 1946, remaining in the post as organist and choir master until his retirement in 1996, at the grand age of 81. Herrick is buried in the Dean Cemetery.

The Rieger organ was installed in 1992 and built by the Austrian firm of Rieger Orgelbau, in consultation with Herrick Bunney and Peter Hurford.

The instrument has a highly distinctive case of Austrian oak, designed by Douglas Laird. There aren't many organs that lend themselves to a proper rendition of Olivier Messiaen's 'La Nativité du Seigneur' and there have been a few notable performances of this sublime work here since the organ was installed.

I had difficulty mustering up the concentration to capture this photograph, owing to being spell-bound by the view of the square that can be seen here. It is difficult to believe that this scene was photographed on a Saturday afternoon in May.

You could come here at 4.30 on a June morning and capture a shot like this with no traffic or people anywhere. Yes indeed, but not with the sun shining on it like this.

ST GILES CATHEDRAL

43

VICTORIA TERRACE AND VICTORIA STREET

If the walls of Victoria Terrace could speak of legends past we can only imagine what eerie tales might arise from this scene in the Old Town of Auld Reekie.

Although there is a 'Carnaby Street' ambience nowadays, the same could not be said of life here in past centuries. Poverty, disease and neglect would have been all too obvious to the passer-by.

In the 21st century, fine wine and sumptuous cuisine can be enjoyed in and out of doors along this terrace, in sunlight and in moonlight; and looking down to Victoria Street below there's a myriad of antique shops, bars and markets ready to greet tourist and city resident alike. You cannot be a visitor in Edinburgh without coming here.

Down below, number 40 Victoria Street is the official site for J.K. Rowling's Harry Potter merchandise. The steep curvature of this street, also known as West Bow, has an abundance of bars, restaurants with old fashioned shops which some years ago would be called after their owner's names: Robert Cresser, Harry Parry and Cathie's Cauldron, among

others. Anne Parkerfield, my mother's pseudonym, owned an antique shop at number 84, (just down on the left before the corner), until the early 1970s.

When Thomas Hamilton drew up plans to have the old West Bow gutted, as part of the city's 1827 Improvement Act, he did so to improve access points in an around the Old Town. A prolific architect at the time, he was asked to construct Victoria Street

in a kind of Old Flemish style. During construction, many of the medieval buildings were demolished and the striking arches lining the new terrace were transformed into shops and drinking houses.

I took this photograph in black and white to create an impression of what this scene might have looked like centuries ago, and this was made all the easier by the lack of traffic and pedestrians in 21st century dress.

GEORGE HERIOT'S SCHOOL

Edinburgh has the distinction of having more private / independently operated schools than anywhere else in Britain. A quarter of the Capital's children are educated at fee-paying schools.

George Heriot's is located on Lauriston Place in the Old Town and the architecture of the main building is Renaissance, the work of William Wallace in the early 1600s. Note these ravishing turrets which overlook a large quadrangle. The foundation stone is inscribed with the date 1628 and over the centuries there have been many additions, notably the gatehouse by William Henry Playfair, and the chapel by James Gillespie Graham in the 1820s and '30s. There are also some very fine carvings above the windows.

Originally an 'all-boys' school, but mixed gender since the 1980s, it was established in 1628 as the George Heriot Hospital, by bequest of the royal goldsmith George Heriot, and it opened in 1659. On his death (in 1624) Heriot left around twenty-five thousand pounds — equivalent to several tens of millions today which was to be used to found a charitable school / hospital to care for the poor, fatherless children of Edinburgh. The school is governed today by the George Heriot Trust, a Scottish charity.

Due to Edinburgh's hilly terrain this splendid building can be photographed from several different vantage points. I'm standing on Victoria Terrace, overlooking Victoria Street and the Grassmarket.

NATIONAL LIBRARY OF SCOTLAND

The National Library of Scotland on George IV Bridge is a fine example of 1930s architecture by one of the leading architects of the day, Reginald Fairlie. As well as being the world's foremost centre for the study of Scotland and the Scots, it's also a European research library with collections of world-class importance. Anyone can get a library card to consult material in the reading rooms and the collection comprises up to seven million books and over two million maps.

Building work commenced in 1938, was interrupted by the Second World War, and was completed in 1956. It is built on seven floors.

The facade is graced by seven large stone figures by the renowned sculptor, Hew Lorimer.

THE TOMB OF DAVID HUME

I come to the Old Calton Burial Ground cemetery on Waterloo Place and here is the tomb of David Hume, Scottish philosopher and historian. He lived between 1711 and 1776, and studied at both Edinburgh and Glasgow Universities.

Hume was a leading figure in the Scottish Enlightenment and became known all over Europe in the 18th century. He wrote many volumes in a series called 'The History of England', and in his philosophical works he explains that many of our beliefs "do not come from reason. Instead, they come from our instincts or feelings".

The design of this mausoleum, built in 1777, is a typical example of the work of Hume's close friend, architect Robert Adam, and here's what Hume says in his will, regarding his burial:

"I also ordain that, if I shall die anywhere in Scotland, I shall be buried in a private manner in the Calton graveyard, the South Side of it, and a monument be built over my body at an expense not exceeding a hundred pounds, with an inscription containing only my name with the year of my birth and death, leaving it to posterity to add the rest".

Hume lived in Edinburgh, on the corner of St David Street and St Andrew Square.

This is a fascinating place, and there are tombs and stone carvings in memory of many dignified names, as can be seen on the statue and plinth.

THE HIGH COURT

Lothian Buses' Volvo B5TL / Wright Gemini 3 number 403 (BN64 CPE) is seen at the High Court on a sunny Saturday afternoon in May. A small number of bus services operated during the pandemic and here's a Service 27 on a thirty minute frequency.

On the ninth week of the coronavirus restrictions there were very few people in the city centre, and this was perhaps a safer place to take a walk, compared to the leafy parks and ponds which were busier.

The High Court was designed by architect John Wilson Paterson and completed in 1937. This building was originally Edinburgh Sheriff Court, and became the High Court in 1994. The intention was to keep the facade of the building, and the surrounding building quadrangle, in harmony with the classical architecture of Edinburgh which accounts for: those giant Doric columns, a pedimented centrepiece, rusticated ashlar stone on the ground floor, and stone balustrades with corniced eaves. These were New Town features that William Henry Playfair and his contemporaries would have approved of a century earlier in the early 1800s.

The sculpture is of the philosopher David Hume, (1711 -1776), which was completed in 1996 by Sandy Stoddart.

HUME AND THE PIPER

A piper in Highland dress plays to a deserted High Street.

For those who walk, drive or travel in public transport, Hume's statue feels as though it has occupied this position for a very long time. Stoddart has enjoyed the title of 'Queen's Sculptor in Ordinary in Scotland' since 2008, and first came to fame in the 1980s with statues in both Glasgow and Edinburgh.

This statue brought fame to Stoddart and he went on to present the Capital with another great work, that of Scottish mathematical physicist James Clerk Maxwell, at the east end of George Street (see pages 78 and 79).

GRASSMARKET

Lying in a hollow of the Old Town, the Grassmarket gets its name from being a market place. Traditionally, this would have been a gathering place for market traders and cattle dealers. Today, maintaining the same traditions, it boasts fine taverns and hotels.

In the 21st century there are modern day markets here, with fine dining being the order of the day within the many restaurants on either side of the square.

I am here on a Saturday afternoon, on the seventh week of the coronavirus restrictions and we can observe Edinburgh, the silent city — asleep, beautifully tranquil and all at rest. I stood here listening to bird song, it seemed louder than ever — the birds above sounding happy at the golden silence everywhere.

COWGATE

The Cowgate is part of the lower level of Edinburgh's Old Town, which, as can be seen from looking along to the tunnel, lies below the elevated streets of South Bridge and George IV Bridge. It was once a dark and gloomy road, due to all the horse muck and industrial smoke but one with a glorious history. I'm standing at the intersection of Candlemaker Row (to the right) and the Grassmarket (behind).

The street's name is recorded from the 1400s and this comes from the medieval practice of herding cattle down the street on market days. A number of other streets in the Old Town of Edinburgh, such as the Grassmarket and Lawnmarket, are named for similar reasons.

On a sunny day it is a pleasure to breathe in the refreshing air quality, and to imagine this scene as it might have been hundreds of years ago.

GREYFRIARS BOBBY

Greyfriars Bobby lived to a grand old age, from 1855 until 1872. He was a Skye Terrier who became known in 19th century Edinburgh for spending fourteen years guarding the grave of his owner until he died himself. Several books and films have been made about him and he has become one of the Capital's most endearing icons.

Bobby belonged to a man called John Gray, who worked for the city's police force as a nightwatchman. When he died he was buried in Greyfriars Kirkyard, just behind the pub here. Bobby then became known locally, spending the rest of his life sitting on his master's grave.

His statue is a massive tourist attraction on George IV Bridge and it's a 'must' for visitors to have their photograph taken with Bobby. It was made by William Brodie RSA, in 1871, and unveiled as a drinking fountain two years later. Brodie also created the Genius of Architecture statue in West Princes Street Gardens (see pages 66 and 67).

CENTRAL LIBRARY

Edinburgh's Central Library on George IV Bridge opened in 1890 and was the first public library in the city. It actually comprises of six libraries: Lending, Reference, Music, Art and Design, Edinburgh and Scottish, and the Children's Library.

This French Renaissance-styled design is by George Washington Browne, with the foundation stone being laid in 1887. His design was the winning entry in an architectural competition for the new library and it was selected from thirty-seven submissions.

It has always been quite common for competitions to be held for public building developments so that architects are able to compete for the prize.

This grand building stands three levels tall above George IV Bridge and reaches down to the Cowgate below.

Above the main door is the motto 'Let there be Light' and instructions were given that this would be inscribed above the entrance to all public libraries in Edinburgh thereafter.

When I was a teenager I would travel in the bus to the library's Music Department. My music case would be filled with several piano scores which my teacher, Sheila Desson-Emslie, had told me to get, using those little orange cardboard tickets we all loved! With her help, I learned several pieces, (around Grade 8 level), every week and was so enlightened by her guidance. As a professional musician I would not be the player and teacher I am today without Sheila's inspirational help and friendship.

The ornamented facade is decorated with stone carvings depicting the coat of arms of the City of Edinburgh, the Coat of Arms of Scotland, and the Royal Arms.

The photograph was taken at midday on a Thursday in May, and this calm and tranquil scene is not perhaps typical of George IV Bridge on a normal week day!

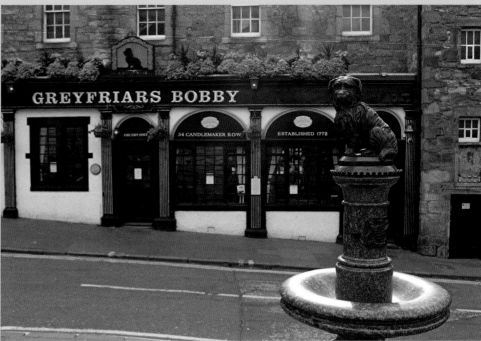

BLACK WATCH

This is The Black Watch, a bronze memorial statue standing on the corner of Market Street and North Bank, at the top of Edinburgh's Mound.

It depicts a soldier in highland dress, dedicated 'To the memory of officers, non-commissioned officers and men of The Black Watch who fell in the South African War 1899 -1902'.

Oh, how silent it was standing here to take this photograph, a very unique silence.

NEWHAVEN

The small harbour at Newhaven is used mainly by pleasure craft; and there's something very soothing about standing on a harbour watching the boats move to the rhythm of the waves.

The octagonal lighthouse was built in the 1890s and remains in good condition. It stands as a reminder to the once vibrant fishing industry.

Newhaven was once a village and harbour with a registered population of around five thousand. Until around 1900, Newhaven was a major port for landing oysters and it also played a role in the whaling industry, at 'Whale Brae' at the north end of Newhaven Road.

The houses in the main street are typical of many Scottish villages, with each originally having a staircase leading up to accommodation on the first floor, the ground floor being used for storing nets. Some of the more modern housing seen here dates from the 1960s and has replicated the older style of building. Originally, the village would have looked out over the Firth of Forth, but today it is surrounded by modern housing and small industrial developments. It was

once connected by the Leith North Branch of the Caledonian Railway, but the line closed in 1962.

At the far end the big white building is Chancelot Flour Mill, on the south side of Western Harbour, built in the 1970s.

One of Edinburgh's most famous restaurants was called The Peacock Inn. Its entrance was on the other side of these houses at the far end on the main road. It served traditional high teas and suppers that were renowned. Fish and chips was their speciality dish which came in different sizes, including one called the 'Whale'.

NEW COLLEGE ON THE MOUND

New College is today the home of the Church of Scotland, but originally it was built for the Free Church. An annual Assembly is held here in the month of May.

Following the Disruption in the Church of Scotland in 1843, the emergent Free Church urgently required a new theological college in Edinburgh, an Assembly Hall and a home for the Free High Church.

This is another creation from the offices of William Henry Playfair, from 1846, with the Assembly Hall being designed by David Bryce in 1858/59.

It is interesting to compare the architectural style of this building to Playfair's RSA and National Gallery, just sixteen years separate them apart but observe the Gothic features of New College. It clearly demonstrates how styles were changing and how architects wished to further their careers with new ideas.

The building was used as the Scottish Parliament, following Devolution in 1999, until the designated building at Holyrood was completed in 2004.

The photograph was taken in mid-evening during May with the sun far round in the north-west. Only for a few weeks in summer months is New College graced with sunlight on its facade.

Note the absence of people walking about and what pleasure it was not to have any parked vehicles in front of the building.

WILLIAM PITT

The statue of William Pitt (the younger) stands at the intersection of Frederick Street and George Street. It was erected in 1833.

Pitt was the youngest ever Prime Minister of the United Kingdom, elected at the age of twenty-four, and serving in office between 1783 and 1801 and 1804 to 1806. He was also Chancellor of the Exchequer for the entire period when he was Prime Minister and is most remembered for his financial abilities following the war for American independence, which ended in 1783.

He restructured taxation, for example reducing the duty on tea from 119% to 12% but increasing the 'Window Tax', which had been introduced to Scotland in 1748 and was paid on the number of windows over seven. It is often said that because New Town houses had more windows than other districts this was a reason to block some with stone slabs, but it is likely that this was in fact done to achieve architectural symmetry.

I am standing in the middle of the road on a weekday afternoon.

THE BALMORAL CLOCK

The time on the clock is just after twenty-five minutes past six.

Fifty-eight metres in height, rich in late romantic ornamentation and with an international reputation, this is Edinburgh's equivalent of Big Ben in London.

The design for the North British Hotel's clock tower came from the pen of one of my favourite architects, William Hamilton Beattie. In 1895 he was asked to enter a competition to construct a landmark building for the east end of Princes Street. The North British Railway told him they wanted a very grand hotel for Waverley railway station beneath.

Work began on Beattie's design in 1896 and it opened in 1902. Sadly, he died before it was completed and he rests, along with several other members of his family, in the Old Dean Cemetery. He did, however, see the completion of his other great masterpieces in Edinburgh, Jenners on Princes Street, and Patrick Thomson's department store, now the Hilton Edinburgh Carlton Hotel, at the top of the North Bridge.

Oh, how I adore clock faces, and just look at the size of these metal hands on the four-faced cube, pointing in all directions of the compass, and with those Roman numerals. With such silence all around me, I'd swear I could hear the giant pendulum ticking inside!

This kind of photograph works well when there is a clear blue sky as a backdrop.

EDINBURGH TRAMS

The story of Edinburgh's Trams has had its ups and downs since construction began in 2008. Extensive disputes and delays in the building of the near to nine miles of tramway, between Edinburgh Airport and York Place in the centre of town, together with the disruptive upheaval of the city centre, meant that it did not open until 2014, at a cost of seven hundred and seventy-six million pounds (initially the estimation was for three hundred and seventy-five million pounds).

There are sixteen stops along the route. Despite the service operating almost identically to the express bus service 100, (in duration and distance), it has been popular with passengers who travel east to west and vice versa within the city centre, and also with visitors travelling to and from the airport.

On the 31st of May 2014 I met up with Frank and a few other acquaintances at the Gyle Centre, where the first tram in Edinburgh since 1956 would start from. The time was around 5.30am and there were many people gathering. I was really excited and stood at the edge of the platform, hoping that the tram would stop and that the door would open in front of me. My wish was granted, but then — cue the drum roll! — my jaw dropped as I saw a large camera looking right at me. I was about to appear on the BBC's Breakfast Time and within half an hour I was receiving telephone texts at the rate of one every couple of minutes. My moment of fame, being on television!

In 2019, the City of Edinburgh Council voted to approve the extension of the line from York Place to Newhaven, and this is estimated to be completed by 2023.

During the coronavirus restrictions trams continued to operate, but on a thirty minute service.

BRISTO BAPTIST CHURCH

Dominant and bold, this Scandinavian style building is home to the Bristo Baptist Church at the top of Orchard Brae.

Built by William Paterson of Oldrieve in the 1930s, his plan was to create an L-shape design to fit the road pattern. The tall shaped gable of the church looking downhill, with its arcaded Corinthian-columned porch and High Renaissance window, is eye-catching. In this photograph the church towers over an unusually quiet Queensferry Road.

The great American Baptist evangelist, Billy Graham had both a huge impact and following all over the world until his death in 2018, at the age of ninety-nine. Throughout his long life his fervent aspiration was to tour as many countries as he could, and in 1955 he embarked on a massive tour of Britain, which included a sixteen day mission to preach services at the Kelvin Hall gallery in Glasgow. In the 1990s Graham held a rally at Murrayfield stadium which many thousands attended.

COMELY BANK AVENUE

What a wonderful view and I'm standing on Dean Park Crescent, looking all the way to Ferry Road. On the distant left-hand side within those trees is Fettes College School which is beside Broughton High, home to the City of Edinburgh Music School. On the right in the distance is Inverleith Park.

When I was little I was given a pedal car, a white Bentley type thing which had a red interior. I loved to seek out hills to race down and had lots of fun on the small gradient at the top of St. Bernard's Crescent. I was a bit of a tear-away and would often scare the living daylights out of people who were walking up the pavement, while I was racing down towards them in my pedal car, also on the pavement! I'm sure my mum was constantly apologising to the neighbours for my shocking behaviour, but what fun I was having.

Eventually the car became scratched with all the bumps I was giving it, and then one day it disappeared and I never saw it again. I think my dad decided I was getting too big for it and enough was enough!

I am standing at the top of this hill at Comely Bank Avenue and imagining the fun I could have had on these pavements in my little car then!

CARLTON STREET

Carlton Street is part of the Raeburn Estate and, along with its neighbouring streets, was designed by James Milne.

Henry Raeburn was born in Stockbridge and in 1780 he married Ann Edgar (widow of Count James Leslie) and both were acknowledged in the naming of Ann Street and Leslie Place nearby. The development was built at the end of the Georgian New Town era between 1813 and 1826.

Raeburn lived in St. Bernard's House until his death in 1823; the house thereafter being demolished to make way for the new Carlton Street. Unlike the adjacent Danube Street, with its pavilioned curvature at the north end, Carlton Street is perfectly straight.

Note the impressive rusticated stone work on the ground floors and the glorious drawing room flats on the first floors. These would originally have been complete town houses but over the centuries have been converted into flats, the drawing room level being the finest with those magnificent long windows. The balustrades on both sides of the street and balconies along the central portion give this short terrace an impressive appearance.

The Charlotte lanterns are relatively new, these days lighting up many New Town streets, and were partly paid for by the residents of the street in the 1980s. At the far end is St. Bernard's Crescent and Leslie Place.

I had great pleasure for many years as a little boy regularly visiting my grandparents who owned a drawing room flat here, (on the other side out of shot), a fine address at which my father and two uncles also resided.

ANTONY GORMLEY

We're on the bridge at Stockbridge, looking down on the Water of Leith at this self sculpture of Antony Gormley standing in the water. There are six of these in Edinburgh, entitled The Six, and how perfectly life-like they look.

British sculptor Sir Antony Mark David Gormley OBE, was born in 1950 and his most famous work is the Angel of the North in Gateshead. It was erected in February 1998 and is considered one of the finest sculptures in the world. In 2008 The Daily Telegraph ranked Gormley number four in their list of the 'one hundred most powerful people in British culture'.

It is interesting to observe people's reactions when they see this sculpture of Gormley and everybody looks once, and then fixes their eyes a second time due to the life-like appearance of this and his other art pieces in natural settings.

The other five sculptures of Gormley can be seen at: Powderhall, Bonnington, Ocean Terminal, and there are two at the Gallery of Modern Art.

GULLS ON INVERLEITH POND

During the coronavirus restrictions sea gulls lived off a thin diet without the usual chip wrappers and sandwiches to nibble on — foods that have brought them into city centres over the years, where in former times they would have stayed at home by the sea.

At Inverleith Park here they are having a great party together and probably feeling like a few tasty snacks. One or two gave me pleading looks, but whilst on my local walk I certainly wasn't going to part with my chocolate bar!

STEWART AND BALFOUR IN 'KIDNAPPED'

Neatly positioned on Corstorphine Road, near to Saughtonhall, stands this memorial to Robert Louis Stevenson depicting the two principal characters from his book 'Kidnapped' — Alan Breck Stewart and David Balfour. Stewart is on the left and Balfour on the right. This was precisely the location in which they took leave of each other.

It was made by Sandy Stoddart, creator of the David Hume statue outside the High Court, and also more recently of James Clerk Maxwell at the east end of George Street. Sean Connery unveiled this statue in 2004.

Read this paragraph from 'Kidnapped', written in 1886. "We came the by-way over the hill from Corstorphine, and when we got near to the place called Rest-and-be-Thankful, and looked down on Corstorphine bogs and over to the city and the castle on the hill, we both stopped, for we both knew without a word said that we had come to where our ways parted".

THE CANONMILLS CLOCK

The time is just after twenty-one minutes past seven, on a warm spring evening.

One of the things that attracted me to come and live in Canonmills was this clock. A high street or village isn't complete without a central clock and I often feel sad when I visit modern developments that there are often no focal points to admire: a church, for example, or a pub, a newsagent, or a clock.

Erected in 1945, the clock was gifted by Archibald G. Bryson, Session Clerk of St. Mary's Parish Church. It was designed by Leslie Grahame Thomson, with the movement made by James Ritchie and Son on Dundas Street.

It is often noted that the clock, which doesn't chime, runs three minutes fast in order to allow the post office, (seen to the left), to close early. Who knows if that's true, but it's a nice story!

WEST PRINCES STREET GARDENS

One of my favourite places to visit during the 2020 coronavirus pandemic was West Princes Street Gardens. Normally, on a nice sunny day there are many other people enjoying the delights of this garden and it can often become a little crowded. With only a few people taking local exercise and just a few tourists it was joyous to come here.

The statue by William Brodie is entitled 'The Genius of Architecture', depicting a goddess placing laurel wreaths on the heads of two boys who appear to be wearing kilts. It was created for the 1862 International Exhibition in London.

Brodie's most popular sculpture in Edinburgh is Greyfriars Bobby, on George IV Bridge (see pages 48 and 49).

The serenity and peaceful calm in Princes Street Gardens always bring joy to Edinburgh's residents and visitors, especially in summer months. With all the marvels of 21st century technology at our fingertips I would like to think the young man sitting on the bench there, gazing into his smart phone, is selecting something to

watch and to listen to that might reflect the beautiful haven of tranquillity that surrounds him. One can only guess, but it might very well be something like Handel's 'Where 'er you walk', or something else soothing, to compliment the warm sunshine that everyone is enjoying in this scene.

For me, in a magical place like this, I prefer to hear the rustling of the trees, the singing of the birds and the wind blowing around me.

MONUMENT TO SIR WALTER SCOTT

This stone tower is a Victorian Gothic monument dedicated to Scottish author Sir Walter Scott. Following Scott's death in 1832 Sir John Steell was commissioned to design a monumental statue in commemoration, and the foundation stone was laid in 1840. The tower was completed by the autumn of 1844, at a cost of just over sixteen thousand pounds.

The tower is over two hundred feet high and has several 'open' viewing galleries reached by a series of narrow spiral staircases, offering panoramic views of Edinburgh and its surroundings. The highest viewing deck is reached by a total of two hundred and eighty-seven steps and those who climb them can obtain a certificate commemorating their efforts. But the top portion is essentially for fit people who are also slim. There's a rare view from every part of this monument and the pleasure of going to the top is nothing short of thrilling.

The statue is of David Livingstone (1813-1873), Scottish physician and pioneering missionary who had a passionate ambition to explore Africa. He was one of the most popular British heroes of the Victorian era.

CRANES ON LEITH STREET

For many people, building site cranes are of great interest and there's a plethora of them for the building of the new hotel complex and retail centre on Edinburgh's Leith Street, replacing the King James Hotel and St. James Centre.

On this sunny day, how their contours and gyrating angles stand out against a blue sky in such a striking manner — different every time they move of course — and at night their fascinating illuminated red lights can be seen for miles.

THE SCOTTISH PARLIAMENT

The site at the foot of the historic Royal Mile was chosen for Scotland's new parliament building. This followed a referendum in 1997 when the people of Scotland voted for the creation of the first Scottish Parliament in almost three hundred years. The four-acre site is next to the Royal Palace of Holyrood House and Holyrood Park. When chosen as the new site it was, at that time, occupied by a Scottish and Newcastle brewery.

The official inauguration of the new Parliament building took place on the 9th of October 2004 in the presence of the Queen, although construction was not completed until April 2005.

Seen from high up on Arthur's Seat the rooves of the parliament have the form of upturned boats. This was a key feature of the design by architect Enric Miralles who died in 2000, aged forty-five, a few months after construction on the building commenced.

Donald Dewar also died in 2000. He was Secretary of State for Scotland and then First Minister in the Scottish Parliament. It was he who selected the Holyrood site and also Miralles as principal architect for the project.

I think this is the best place from which to see our Scottish Parliament building and at the same time to admire all the beauty around it.

THE (former) ROYAL HIGH SCHOOL

The former Royal High School is a 19th century neo-classical building on Regent Road, below Calton Hill. After the school was vacated in 1968 the building was refurbished to accommodate a new devolved legislature for Scotland.

However, the 1979 devolution referendum failed to provide sufficient backing for a devolved assembly, and subsequently it has been used as offices by Edinburgh City Council, including The Duke of Edinburgh's Award and the Sports and Outdoor Education unit.

Much controversy surrounds this building today as conflicting planning applications are the subject of ongoing debate.

The A-listed building was erected between 1826 and 1829 as part of Edinburgh's Acropolis, at a cost of thirty-four thousand pounds. It was created in the Greek Doric style by well-known New Town architect Thomas Hamilton who designed other streets in the Georgian district of the Capital, including Howe Street where he owned an entire property at number 9.

THE TUN ON HOLYROOD ROAD

It is good to see modern buildings emerge in any city and Edinburgh has had several award winning designs in recent decades, but not all of them have received approval from residents and visitors to the Capital.

The Tun on Holyrood Road, near to the Scottish Parliament building, breaks with tradition in shape and colour, and has received a mixed reception since its opening in 2002. The site housed a former Scottish and Newcastle brewery and was redeveloped during the mid-1990s.

'Allan Murray Architects' presented plans for a versatile building which would include offices for the World Wildlife Fund and BBC Scotland. The BBC's relocation from 5 Queen Street was announced in 1999 and the new studios opened here three years later.

In 1999 John McCormick, BBC Scotland's Controller, said the new base would offer "an improved BBC presence which would also provide the flexible, creative workspace required to meet our future broadcasting needs". However, it was concluded a few years after opening that the premises were really too small for what was required, compared to the former studio in Queen Street. It is considerably smaller than the 'state of the art' studios at Pacific Quay in Glasgow.

'Allan Murray Architects' went on to be given the 'Best Commercial Workplace Regional Award' for the Tun building in 2003.

I recall not liking the Tun when it was built, but seen on a sunny day like this, with no traffic or pedestrians on the street, it's powerful and dominant.

LOOKING UP EDINBURGH'S ROYAL MILE

Taken during the eleventh week of coronavirus restrictions, here is a view looking up the Royal Mile from the bottom of the Canongate.

How different everything looks with the complete absence of traffic and people — like looking at an artist's impression of the area before building work began.

ABBEYHILL

I walked down the hill from Regent Road towards Holyrood Palace and the Scottish Parliament on this glorious day in May. I was thinking I might climb Salisbury Crags to get a few aerial photographs, and then I decided to turn round and look back. This is what I saw: a totally deserted road and the railway bridge near to Waverley Station enveloped in a rather rare quietness.

It is very important for us photographers to walk in order to discover opportunities as we go. We cannot do this from behind the wheel of a motor car. Remember also to turn around and look behind you every so often; if you don't, you could be walking away from a golden photo.

55 Abbeyhill was designed by Robert Morham (1839-1912), an Edinburgh based architect who became the City Superintendent of Works in 1873.

Built in 1896 in red sandstone, it's clearly Romanesque in style, not typical of Edinburgh, with castle-like elements, corner turrets and animal figure gargoyles. It was used as a police station until the 1930s.

At the end of the 19th century, this area of Abbeyhill was dominated by heavy industry with a chemical works and two breweries situated close by, and with the railway line running close to Waverley station. Most of the industry has now gone.

In my research I discovered a fascinating story about this building. From the 1980s until 2008 it was an Armenian restaurant called 'Aghtamar Lake Van Monastery in Exile', seemingly well known among locals for its random opening times and highly entertaining owner, Petros Vartynian.

Apparently, he didn't like his diners to arrive late, and would sometimes ask them to help with the washing up. And if you didn't clear your plate you didn't get the next course, according to diners. The restaurant was lit by candlelight and the ambience was very memorable.

For years this restaurant was considered very special, but trying to make a booking was, to say the least, a great achievement. You could however devour some amazing food which would often take the form of a ten-course Armenian banquet that diners raved about.

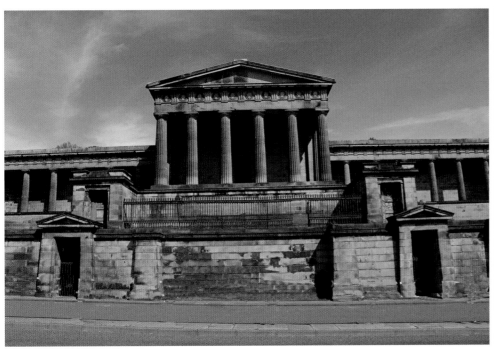

MEMORIAL TO ROBERT BURNS

Regent Road at twelve noon on Wednesday the 20th of May 2020. This was another day when the sun shone brilliantly and temperatures in Edinburgh reached twenty-four degrees. What an astonishing scene to observe with no people or traffic. I might as well have been standing here at five in the morning.

Robert Burns lived in Edinburgh for two years, from 1786. This most ravishing masterpiece was created by Thomas Hamilton. The Burns memorial with its Corinthian columns harks very much back to the Greek temples of old; and in celebration of the Arts, this joyous structure is modelled on the ancient Choragic monument of Lysicrates, in Athens.

By the mid-1830s there was a desire among architects to move away from the classical symmetry so typical of central Edinburgh, and Hamilton worked in a group who developed a new 'Gothic' style. Working in this style, he was responsible for the North Free Church on George IV Bridge, which fell into disuse in the 1930s and then became the Bedlam theatre around 1980.

HERIOT ROW

Heriot Row is one of the most beautiful streets in Edinburgh's New Town, the city's planned, and phased, expansion to the north, during the period of the Scottish Enlightenment. It was the first street in the New Town's second phase.

Several of Heriot Row's first residents were significant figures in the 19th century, including writer Robert Louis Stevenson, (at number 17 along there on the right), but almost every house has interesting tales to tell of cultured and enterprising residents.

All my favourite architectural delights can be seen here as we look along the row, designed by Robert Reid. The central pediment is based on Robert Adam's centrepiece in Charlotte Square, but look how neat and restrained everything is, not shouting out in the name of grandeur. There are just two raised floors above ground level and you can see how the stonework has retained its durability, two hundred years on.

Observe the rustic ashlar stonework on the ground floors, the mouchette fanlights, simple iron balconies on the first floors and long and elegant drawing room windows. At both ends there are three tenement entrances which form the 'pavilion' theme typical of the style.

THE CALEY PICTURE HOUSE

Situated on Lothian Road, the Caley picture house was one of over forty cinemas in Edinburgh. The auditorium opened in 1923 and in its original form seated nine hundred, which, by 1928, was increased to nearly two thousand.

The cinema was closed in 1984 and shortly after was converted into a discothèque. Notable past performers included Robin Trower, Wishbone Ash, Uriah Heep, Hawkwind, Rory Gallagher, Queen, Beck, Bogert & Appice, Gentle Giant and AC/DC — (I think I have heard of a few of them!).

The building became a Wetherspoons bar in 2016.

PATERSON'S LAND

On a very silent Holyrood Road this is the front of the University of Edinburgh's Paterson's Land — a major new facility built at the turn of the 20th century to accommodate rising numbers of student teachers and improve training methods.

The architect, Alan K. Robertson, was commissioned to draw up plans for a Teaching Centre for some eight hundred students. A three storey high building of simple classical design was developed with a central quadrangle, entered by gates from Holyrood Road.

Building work on this 'New Training College' started in 1911 and it was ready for use three years later, following the completion of the north-east wing with its rooms for Art, Woodwork and Sewing.

In 1994/95 the building was renamed Paterson's Land, in honour of Dr. Maurice Paterson who had been Rector of the Moray House School from 1864 -1907.

JAMES CLERK MAXWELL

One of the more recent additions to Edinburgh's monuments was unveiled in 2008. This is the work of Alexander Stoddart who also created the David Hume statue outside the High Court in 1996 (see pages 46 and 47). Maxwell was one of Scotland's greatest scientists, and the statue was commissioned in 2006 by the Royal Society of Edinburgh.

Sir James Clerk Maxwell was the founder of electro-magnetic theory, and here he is, sitting admiring the parking meters and buses at the east end of George Street. Sandy Stoddart says "Statues make us realise that communities are made of three components — the living, the dead and those yet to be born", and he goes on to say "they have solemnity, and bring a town to a halt and stop this feverish vibrancy which we are all striving for".

In 2020 we could perhaps learn from Stoddart's words on our continual 'striving for a feverish vibrancy'. Let's hope we can now slow things down just a little.

The photograph, taken mid-afternoon on the last Tuesday in May, demonstrates that Edinburgh is in virtual hibernation.

TRAVERSE THEATRE

I feel that modern buildings need to have space around them to breathe, and to allow the passer-by to admire the depth of the design. Sometimes they appear crushed into an area, squeezed in between older buildings; but the Traverse Theatre in Cambridge Street has a graceful eloquence and doesn't over-power the admirer.

The original Traverse was more of a theatre club venue in the Lawnmarket, founded in 1963 to energise the spirit of the Edinburgh Festival. In those early days it was also used as an exhibition arts centre.

Following a further move in 1969, it was felt that a more prestigious building and location were required and in 1992 it moved to Cambridge Street. The Cambridge Street building, seen here, includes two theatres, and restaurant facilities, making The Traverse a major venue in the Capital.

I think this is an excellent example of modern architecture with a generosity in the use of colour, shape and stonework. Captured on camera on a sunny day like this it attracts the eye from a distance, and importantly it doesn't feel out of place alongside the Usher Hall.

EDINBURGH COLLEGE OF ART

The Edinburgh College of Art is now one of the Schools in the University of Edinburgh. Its history can be traced back to the 1760s, and it has become an international leader in research and research-led teaching in the creative arts, humanities, and creative technologies.

This is the Hunter building, part of the Lauriston Campus which was expanded in 1977 to include this L-shape red sandstone building. On the left is the former Lothian and Borders Fire and Rescue Service with its Museum of Fire, now part of the college.

When I walk up the hill from Tollcross and see this building before me I develop a sense of calm, as if everything falls into place in my mind. It might be the smooth and sweet eloquence of the red sandstone, untypical of the Capital but nonetheless appealing to the eye.

LAURISTON PLACE

Notable buildings on and around Lauriston Place include the Edinburgh College of Art's Lauriston Campus, George Heriot's School, the Royal Infirmary's Lauriston building, Chalmers Hospital and the Princess Alexandra Eye Pavilion (on Chalmers Street).

On the right is the former Royal Infirmary, now being restored and developed by Quartermile, and in the distance the University of Edinburgh's McEwan Hall.

On a sunny summer week day afternoon in June, I was able to walk down the middle of this road and not worry in the least about vehicles coming either way — an astonishing freedom.

TOLLCROSS

The time is ten minutes to four on a Wednesday afternoon in May. It's the eleventh week of coronavirus lockdown and the city of Edinburgh remains in hibernation.

Scotland was exemplary at abiding by the rule 'Stay at Home' and such a scene would be impossible ever to imagine in normal times.

We're looking at what was the site of Edinburgh's Goldberg's department store, oh a long time ago now. The Ritchie clock standard is one of four. Only this one and another at Morningside can be seen these days — the other two are in storage.

The Bank of Scotland is on the left with the Castle ahead, and then High Riggs and Lauriston up to the right. In years to come photographs like this will be timely reminders of this rather strange period in our lives.

THE KING'S THEATRE

Most people in Edinburgh have been to the King's Theatre at some point in their lives, most likely in the Christmas season for the pantomime. It is home to Edinburgh's annual pantomime season, run by Capital Theatres.

This is the moment for some audience participation and you are allowed to shout out....

Oh, no I haven't! or Oh, yes I have!

With its somewhat atypical stonework for Edinburgh, the King's was built as a rival to the successful Royal Lyceum Theatre, which had already been entertaining audiences for twenty years. The architect of the building's exterior was James Davidson who served as the Provost of Coatbridge, and he was responsible for the design of many public buildings in Lanarkshire. The King's therefore represents Davidson's Lanarkshire municipal building design, and is rather unique for the Capital.

Andrew Carnegie laid the foundation stone in 1906 and the theatre opened two years later with a production of Cinderella. Everybody but everybody in the world of theatre entertainment has performed here, notably in our lifetime: Dave Willis, Stanley Baxter, Kenneth McKellar, Rikki Fulton, Jimmy Logan, Dorothy Paul, Una Maclean, Johnny Beattie, Grant Stott, Allan Stewart, Andy Gray and many others.

By the late 1960s theatres all over Britain started to see a decline in audience numbers, probably due to the development of television. Many would have to close or become more versatile in the type of audience they would require if success was to continue.

In 1969 Edinburgh City Council bought the theatre and promised to secure its future, and this would include making it a major venue in the Edinburgh International Festival. It also became home to Scottish Opera for a while. Its rival, the Empire, (now the Festival Theatre), had been converted into a bingo hall and the Playhouse was still being used in the 1970s as a cinema.

A huge restoration programme of work was completed in the 1980s with the construction of wider aisles in the auditorium and a larger orchestra pit. The number of seats was halved, from the original two and a half thousand to thirteen hundred and thirty.

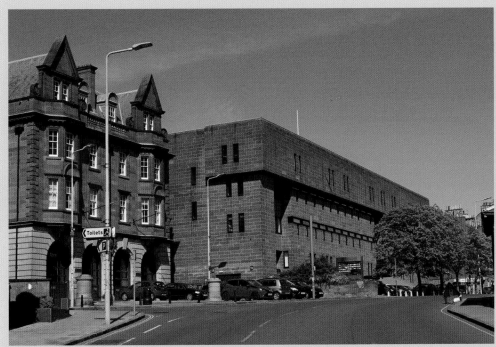

SILVERKNOWES GOLF COURSE

A glorious day, and the reins of lockdown in Scotland start to ease a little. This was Friday the 29th of May when golf courses were allowed to open, and the time had come to polish the clubs and get our technique back up to scratch.

From this day we were allowed to venture a little further than just a 'local' walk; and by travelling up to five miles from home while still observing social distancing we could begin to enjoy a little more freedom.

The first place I wanted to go to was along the promenade at Silverknowes, and here I am on my way at the golf course looking over to Cramond Island.

Oh, how delightfully pleasurable it was to feel the wind and fresh air of the seaside, perfectly joyous.

SAILOR'S COTTAGE, CRAMOND

At the fishing village of Cramond this is the little tea room where you can see a selection of fine paintings by local artists while also enjoying some hot soup with home-made bread, a cup of tea and a tasty selection of home baking.

We come here on beautiful days like this to enjoy the bracing air of the sea, and I love the way this Sailor's Cottage is kept so well painted in snow-white, with flowering tubs all round.

PONDS IN THE GALLERY OF MODERN ART

How nice to be able to meander around the grounds of the Gallery of Modern Art during the lockdown restrictions; and these newly created ponds have made the area in front of the gallery a tranquil and green space to enjoy.

THE GULLS ARE BACK

During the coronavirus pandemic there was a notable absence of seagulls in the centre of Edinburgh. I feel they are out of place in the middle of a city, rather that they belong at the seaside. I suppose though that one might consider, for the most fleeting of moments, that our city could have been called Edinburgh-On-Sea, as we are somewhat near the Firth of Forth!

Perhaps it's those careless people who leave their litter and unfinished chip-wrappers that bring these hungry birds so close to the town, but I wouldn't have wanted to be eating an ice cream cone with these three watching me today!

THE CALEDONIAN HOTEL

A scene to take the breath away! Lothian Road on a sunny Saturday morning, just after the eleventh hour on the eleventh week of the coronavirus lockdown.

I had to muster up all my concentration to position myself for this photograph, such was my sense of bewilderment at the stillness all around me. However, I didn't have to worry as nothing in the way of traffic materialised for several minutes.

On such a sunny summer's morning it was joyous to be here alone. I have always wanted to get a picture with the sun shining on the Caley Hotel — such opportunities to do this present themselves only in the morning, but trying to capture a good photo is usually impossible owing to the plethora of buses, cars, cyclists and pedestrians.

Using its title today, Waldorf Astoria Edinburgh, this is a five-star hotel which opened in 1903. It is an example of a grand railway hotel, formerly called The Caledonian, nicknamed 'The Caley'.

It was constructed from 1899 to 1903 and was part of the Caledonian Railway's Edinburgh Princes Street Station. It was a rival to the North British Hotel which opened at the east end of Princes Street in 1902. The hotel was built on top of the stone built, V-shaped station which replaced the previous wood-built station that was damaged in a fire in 1890. The architects were John Peddie and George Washington Browne. (Washington Browne also designed Edinburgh's Central Library in George IV Bridge (see pages 48 and 49).

In 1965, Princes Street Station closed and was demolished by 1970. This provided room for expansion for the hotel, and the cast-iron gates at the entrance to the car park in Rutland Street are the only reminder of the station. The original station clock, pre-dating the fire of 1890, has been preserved inside the hotel.

ST. GEORGE'S WEST CHURCH

Whenever I pass this church on Shandwick Place I want to stop and stare for a few minutes.

St. George's West (now Charlotte Chapel) has a special place in my heart. My mum and dad, George and Nancy were married here, and it was also the church where I was baptised. It was my parish when I was growing up and I have played the organ and given many a recital within its sanctuary. I will never forget the two great legends who reigned here at the same time, between the 1960s and '80's: the Reverend Bill Cattanach DD in the pulpit and Doctor Frank Thomas at the organ — what a wonderful inspiration they were together, in words and music.

Building of the church was completed in 1869, and it was designed by local architect David Bryce, (he is buried in the New Calton Burial ground). There are several admirable features: notably the rose window (out of shot) and also this fine clock tower. The church holds the great honour of having had Doctor Alfred Hollins as its musical director — a mighty composer and organ recitalist; blind from birth he was awarded an Honorary Doctorate by the University of Edinburgh in 1922.

Hollins had a busy concert schedule, touring all over the world, and legend recalls that when the assistant minister of the Free St George's Church, the Reverend Hugh Black, heard Hollins play the organ in Nottingham, he offered him the post here in Edinburgh - a position which he held for the rest of his life, until 1942.

Chiming clocks are becoming less common in cities these days, and owing to increased noise levels those that do chime are sometimes difficult to hear. The bells of St. George's West were once strong enough to peel out over everything for miles, and their vibrant Westminster chimes could be heard across the city every fifteen minutes — every part of Edinburgh could hear this clock, depending on the wind direction.

ST. CUTHBERT'S CHURCH

It is generally accepted that there is no trace remaining of the original St. Cuthbert's Church on Lothian Road, of which the first records appear from the 12th century, but history dictates that in all probability it was founded by Malcolm Canmore and Queen Margaret.

Only the west tower remains of a reconstruction of the church in the 1770s. The clock tower, with its fine steeple, was added in 1789 and the remainder of the church was built in the 1890s, designed by the architect H. J. Blanc.

Wander through the ancient cemetery and you will come across many notable names from centuries past. On this day I spotted the stone of the architect Robert Reid (1819-1888) who, as we have discussed elsewhere, worked extensively on streets and buildings in the New Town.

I am greatly interested in cemeteries and often like to walk through them, admiring the myriad of grave-stones, observing also dates and styles of inscriptions. In places like this you never walk far without stumbling across someone famous. The sense of mystery is intriguing.

QUEENSFERRY STREET

At the start of the coronavirus restrictions I took a photograph here on Queensferry Street. Eleven weeks later I returned to find the very same deserted scene — the only difference being a beautiful blue sky.

25 MELVILLE STREET

In the early 1800's Robert Brown drew up plans to develop Melville Street and this would become part of the Walker Estate; a street with the name Walker is close by.

By 1825 the street was complete and the estate would be owned by Sir Patrick Walker, based on Brown's original plans. In the 1820s Melville Street was described as a 'high class residential scheme' and is the centre and most prestigious street of the estate.

Number 25 faces along Stafford Street and was designed as a five-storey townhouse. It is the most prominent building in this Georgian terrace and today is a combination of offices to rent and converted flats. Note the four Ionic columns and elegant arched window surrounds on the ground floor and I do like the stone balconies on the first floor, which add a touch of panache to this grand address.

I own the green Beetle parked all alone in the street on this sunny day.

KIRK BRAE HOUSE AND THE DEAN BRIDGE

The Scottish Baronial house on the edge of the Dean Bridge has five floors. Three of them are below the bridge. The original part of the house was built in the 1680s, associated with the flour mill in the valley below, named Baxter's House.

Thomas Telford was the architect of the masterpiece design of the Dean Bridge, built in the 1830s. At that time this was one of just two entries to the North of the city centre, the other being the serpentine shaped road between South East Circus Place and North West Circus Place, near to Stockbridge. It spans the Dean gorge one hundred and ten feet over the Water of Leith.

This was one of Telford's last major projects, completed at the age of 73.

When I was little, I would cross this bridge each week to go to my piano lesson with the renowned Mary Moore at 14 Ainslie Place. My mum always made sure I was smartly dressed, my hair brushed and my duffle coat neatly buttoned.

I trotted along the right-hand side here clutching my music case and would often say to myself: 'When I grow up I will be able to see what's over this wall'. Well, that day eventually came and I remember standing on tip toes, clinging on to the little spikes on top of the wall, and being quite wonderstruck by what I saw: a beautiful garden, (the Dean Gardens), and, oh look, a swing! I have always loved swings and even today I like to 'have a go' on them, (as long as there's nobody watching!).

GAYFIELD HOUSE

Wander through the New Town from west to east and you realise when arriving in London Street that that's about all there is left of Georgian architecture. And then you continue along to East London Street, passing Victorian and modern developments towards the bus depot on Annandale Street, and you come across this detached house.

Gayfield House was built by William Butler in the 1760s as a country villa, once probably surrounded by fields and orchards. It belonged originally to Thomas, Lord Erskine, eldest son of the Earl of Mar. After Erskine's death it was sold to the Earl of Leven, and later it became a veterinary college in the 1870s.

Looking at this house in more detail, I rather like those three urns marking out the contours of the central pediment. The handsome portico is held up by a pair of Corinthian columns. All the windows have astragal frames and just to give it little more grandeur it's elevated by these steps up to a front garden.

That arched iron gate at the entrance is crying out, I think, for someone to cultivate a rose bush around its curvature.

How perfect in proportion everything is, and a joy to look at.

ST. MARK'S UNITARIAN CHURCH

The Edinburgh Unitarian Congregation was founded in 1776, the same year as it was established in the United States of America, as a Society of Universalist Dissenters. St. Mark's was built in 1835 as their sixth place of worship.

Early places of worship included the Unitarian Chapel in Young Street. Look up at the head of the building here for the text "There is one God and one mediator between God and man, the man Christ Jesus".

It is probably accurate to say that most musicians in Edinburgh have performed here in Castle Terrace. Over the past half century or so St. Mark's has been a hub for professional and amateur performers: solo recitalists, orchestras and chamber ensembles, competition festivals and lecture recitals.

In the Edinburgh Festival Fringe there can be up to three concerts a day inside these doors and in the 1970s and '80s this was the beloved festival home of the orchestra Philomusica, led by one of Scotland's great violinists and conductors, the late David Hume.

As can be seen, this post-classical building has been squeezed in between more traditional Georgian buildings, and on a slight angle too.

How nice to photograph St. Mark's with no vehicles parked on the street.

DRUMMOND PLACE

This is one part of the Georgian development of Drummond Place, designed by Robert Reid in the first decade of the 19th century. There is much to admire in Drummond Place with its central garden, whin-sett paved surrounds and railings.

The photograph shows one of the pavilioned corner buildings with its additional storey. Note the magnificent quality of the stonework, (from the Craigleith quarry), along this curve of the street. Drummond Place has all the typical features of the day: polished ashlar, pediments. astragal window frames, mouchette fanlights and, as in much of the area, a granite road surface of whin-setts, (what some refer to as 'cobbles').

LEITH TRAM DEPOT

On week 13 of the coronavirus restrictions it became harder to capture photographs like this one on Leith Walk.

This was once the office of Leith tram depot, built in 1938 as part of a renovation project. The main depot itself was a huge structure with a steel and glass roof, and four wide doors at the front. When Leith and Edinburgh amalgamated, and the Edinburgh trams were converted to electric in 1922/23, the Leith depot was enlarged to accommodate more trams.

There were two entrances/exits, one on either side of this building. In tram days both were used in both directions. Probably in bus days a one-way system was used with the buses turning at the back of the depot. Buses always seemed to face the front.

The depot closed to trams in 1956 and to buses in 1976, some time after Marine garage opened at Portobello.

There were several tram depots in Edinburgh: Shrubhill for horse and cable trams and the maintenance of cable and electric; Henderson Row for cable trams; Gorgie, Tollcross, Portobello and Leith, all for electric trams.

Leith was the largest depot in Edinburgh holding over one hundred and fifty trams. Shrubhill was where the horses were stabled, and there were hundreds and hundreds of them.

(Courtesy of Frank Mitchell, Scottish Tramway and Transport Society).

SAUGHTON PARK

Edinburgh Corporation acquired Saughton Park just after the turn of the 20th century and it opened to the public in 1905. It is named in King David the First's charter of 1128 as 'Salectun', the willow farm and it belonged to Holyrood Abbey until 1587, during the reign of Mary, Queen of Scots. By then the name had become Saughtonhall — 'sauch' being a name for 'willow'. There are many willow trees here running along the Water of Leith.

Two wooden bandstands were part of The Scottish National Exhibition, held here in 1908. Once the exhibition was over, the bandstands were taken down and relocated at Portobello's Marine Gardens. In 1909 Edinburgh Corporation felt the bandstand concerts had been so successful they decided to purchase two cast iron Lion Foundry bandstands, one for the Meadows and the other for here at Saughton Park. Concerts continued into the 1970s but sadly, due to neglect, the bandstand fell into considerable disrepair and was dismantled in 1987.

Fortunately, it was put into Edinburgh Council storage, but, its sister, the Meadows bandstand was scrapped in 1953. In 2016 a group of local friends went to see the bandstand at the storage facility. There it was, stacked up on a shelving unit and so plans were drawn up to reinstate it; and a restoration grant was received from the Heritage Lottery Fund. After much hard work, that included recasting several missing pieces, the bandstand is back again in the park, looking quite superb. It is partly looked after by the local community.

I had never before visited Saughton Park in Gorgie, and am grateful to my friends Hugh and Lilian Davidson for making the suggestion. This is a beautiful garden, clearly loved and cared for. Come here and see the well kept herbaceous borders — an inspiration for any gardener, and those who maintain it can take pride in what they have achieved.

The herbaceous peony is typical of the flowers here and if you haven't visited this park before I recommend it highly for a pleasant walk. So peaceful and calm.

JOHN KNOX HOUSE

Protestant reformer John Knox lived here during the 16th century and, although this is considered to be his home, he also resided in Warriston's Close, between the High Street and Cockburn Street.

The house on the corner here was built from the late 1400s and there are many fine features within, including a wooden gallery and a hand-painted ceiling. There are also some fine carvings from the mid-19th century, when extensive restoration took place.

More restoration occurred in the 1980s and there is now a museum within its walls. Today, John Knox House is owned by the Church of Scotland and is used as an administrative centre.

I visited Loch Leven Castle a few years ago, on the little island near Kinross in Fife where Mary, Queen of Scots was detained. There is a plaque on the island stating that the Scottish Queen had asked John Knox to visit her there, in order to discuss the possibility of a greater acceptance, at that time, for Roman Catholicism in Scotland.

NEW CALTON BURIAL GROUND

Where 'er you walk in Edinburgh, your eye is taken by the beauty of its seven hills. This photograph is framed by the magnificent backdrop of Salisbury Crags and the extinct volcano called Arthur's Seat within the Queen's Park at Holyrood. This was described by Robert Louis Stevenson as "a hill for magnitude, a mountain in virtue of its bold design".

Enric Miralles' award winning design for the Scottish Parliament (see pages 70 and 71) rises up from the foot of the Canongate, alongside Holyrood Palace, but here I am within the New Calton Burial Ground — the resting place of many celebrated Edinburgh citizens.

The Old Calton Burial cemetery is in Waterloo Place, opposite the Regent Bridge. The New Calton Burial Ground took over from the old one, around 1820. It can be entered from either Regent Road or Calton Road. Both the old and new burial grounds are parish cemeteries, and the area here was laid out by Thomas Bonnar and completed by Thomas Brown.

Graveyards can inspire in us respect and admiration for those who lived before; and on every path of this steep hill you encounter the names of leading Edinburgh figures, including local architect David Bryce, and the Stevenson plot where several members of the family of Robert Louis Stevenson are buried.

EDINBURGH CITY CHAMBERS

Located opposite St. Giles Cathedral, the City Chambers was originally called the Royal Exchange, designed by architect John Adam in the 1750s.

It was opened by Lord Provost George Drummond in 1760.

The building is surrounded by many small walkways, better known as 'closes'. The Town Council took over part of it in 1811, calling it the City Chambers and then acquired the entire site by the 1890s.

The main building is set back from the High Street, behind a quadrangle, and as can be seen here has an open arcade as its facade.

Note in the central arcade the "Stone of Remembrance", which commemorates residents of Edinburgh who lost their lives in the First World War. This was unveiled by Prince Henry on Armistice Day in 1927.

It was an honour for me to be invited here to receive an award for completing twenty-five years of service in Education with the City of Edinburgh Council.

THE KIRK OF THE CANONGATE

This is Canongate Kirk, in the heart of Edinburgh's Old Town, where Zara Phillips wed Michael Tindall in the summer of 2011. The Kirk has Royal links dating back hundreds of years and Ms. Phillips was said to be 'desperate' to be married in Scotland.

Canongate Kirk, Church of Scotland, serves the parish of the Canongate and also the Palace of Holyrood.

The story of the Kirk on the Royal Mile goes back to medieval times in the 12th century and King David I and to the Coronation of Charles I in the 17th century.

James VII (James II of England) decided in the 1680s that a new building be built near to the Palace of Holyrood. The church was opened in 1690 with a coat of arms of William and Mary above the entrance. Today, Her Majesty Queen Elizabeth II worships here when residing in Holyrood.

Architecturally, the Kirk has a Dutch-style appearance with a most enchanting small Doric-columned portico over the entrance.

The church cemetery is the resting place of the philosopher and economist Adam Smith, the philosopher, (and Smith's biographer), Dugald Stewart and the private secretary of Mary, Queen of Scots.

The statue outside the entrance, erected in 2004, is of Robert Fergusson, an Edinburgh born poet who was said to have influenced Robert Burns. Fergusson lived for only twenty-four years and is buried within the cemetery.

MARY, QUEEN OF SCOTS' BATH HOUSE

Once upon a time — well around 1560 to be precise — Mary, Queen of Scots loved to indulge herself in this, the most famous of bath houses, located behind Holyrood Palace.

It is built on two floors and was once attached to a boundary wall enclosing King James V's privy garden where it sometimes served as a summer house.

In what is probably a fairy story, Scotland's Queen Mary had other ideas for its use, and during her reign she would often come here to bathe in one hundred bottles of the finest French wine. When her ablutions were complete, the wine would then be re-bottled by her servants and, on her own instructions, was presented as a gift to the residents who lived on the High Street.

Some tour bus operators present this story, but rumours that Scotland's Queen was also heard playing the Jew's harp while bathing are firmly denied!

Capturing the bath house in sunlight like this on camera is only possible in high summer when the sun is at this more westerly angle and high enough for it not to be shaded by the buildings and trees nearby. It is also rather fortunate to be able to take the shot without the intrusion of vehicles and pedestrians.

THE QUEEN'S GALLERY

The buildings that today form the Queen's Gallery, alongside Holyrood Palace at the foot of the Canongate, were built in the 1840s with funds being provided by the Duchess of Gordon. When used as a place of worship it was called the Holyrood Free Church and Duchess of Gordon's School. Sadly, it fell into disuse at the end of the 19th century and was then heavily bombed during the Second World War.

The gallery opened in 1962 and was closed for three years from 1999 for extensive alterations, with strict adherence to the original 19th century architecture being enforced. In 2002 Her Majesty Queen Elizabeth II opened the Gallery as part of her Golden Jubilee celebrations.

The Queen's Gallery hosts many exhibitions from the Royal Collection, including paintings and furniture, and there is a fine Royal photographic display which is kept up to date. If you wish to build your collection of Royal memorabilia then this place is a must for everything you desire, and it is open all the year round.

Millions visit this area every year, to view Holyrood Palace, and Enric Miralles' award winning Scottish Parliament opposite.

I came here on a Saturday afternoon around 5pm, with the sun shining all the way down the High Street and Canongate (only possible in high summer) and it felt like the whole area had been cleared of vehicles and people, just for me to take this photo!

OLD MORAY HOUSE, CANONGATE

Old Moray House, almost opposite the Canongate Kirk on the High Street, is the oldest building owned by the University of Edinburgh, and is one of the few remaining original aristocratic buildings in the Canongate.

Designed in the early 1600s by Mary, Countess of Home it was built at a time when the Canongate was becoming a more desirable district for the town houses of the Scottish aristocracy. Its two storeys were created of a light grey freestone and provided an elegant mansion for members of the Countess's family. It has been described by historians as 'the handsomest house in Edinburgh'.

Old Moray House now houses the academic offices of the University's 'Moray House School of Education and Sport'.

How marvellous to stand here on a silent and deserted High Street to take a photo of such a mighty building. To capture it with sunlight flooding its facade the photographer needs to be here after 5pm, (as can be seen from the Old Tolbooth Wynd clock on the immediate left of the picture), and this is only possible in June and July. At other times of the year this side of the High Street stands in a cloak of shade due to the very tall buildings all around.

MARKET STREET

The coronavirus restrictions began on the 23rd of March, with virtually everything in our lives being affected in order to protect us from the deadly virus which, by the beginning of July 2020, had killed more than forty thousand people in the United Kingdom.

For three months we were asked to 'Stay at Home' and 'Save Lives'. The British public obeyed, and our streets remained like Market Street here for thirteen weeks.

I took this photograph on a warm and sunny Saturday afternoon, the 20th of June, and I could hardly believe my eyes that, with restrictions being relaxed a little, such tranquillity and calm still prevailed in our city centre.

I didn't realise that this would probably be the last opportunity I would have to capture photographs like this. From Monday the 22nd of June these scenes were gone and the streets started to become busier with traffic and pedestrians.

The remarkable ambience of 2020 was beginning to come to an end.

ST ANDREW'S HOUSE

Reaching all my length over a wall on East Market Street to capture this scene on camera, we see the newly renovated roof of Waverley Station and a magnificent array of fine architecture on Calton Hill, on this mid-summer's day.

In the centre-right of the photograph is St. Andrew's House, glowing in the afternoon sunshine.

This is the Headquarters of the Scottish Government and stands on the site of the former Calton Jail. The impressive Art Deco building looks out over Waverley station, the Canongate and Holyrood Park.

It was designed by Thomas Tait, of Burnet, 'Tait and Lorne Architects' who won the architectural competition to gain the commission. Construction began in 1935 and was completed four years later.

The official opening ceremony, set to take place on the 12th of October 1939, was cancelled due to the outbreak of the Second World War and instead it was officially opened by King George VI and Queen Elizabeth, on the 26th of February 1940.

WAVERLEY COURT

Waverley Court on East Market Street is home to the City of Edinburgh's Council Headquarters. It was completed by 2007 and designed by Glasgow's 'Building Design Partnership Architects', with the development contract being given to Miller Construction.

Waverley Court is a state-of-the-art creation costing eighty million pounds, bringing together the Council's sixteen hundred customer service staff under one roof.

It is notable for its grass roof terraces, which can be seen from many raised vantage points in the area. The building has several atriums designed to accommodate as much natural light as possible, and its architects wanted to use environmentally friendly materials including natural stone, and to provide plenty of windows.

 The sculpture of the man wearing a white shirt and black trousers is eye-catching, notably for the rainbow coloured tower he stands on. But who is he? 'Everyman' was designed by Stephan Balkenhol in Germany and represents 'Joe Public'.

WAVERLEY BRIDGE

On Saturday the 20th of June the sky was blue and the sun shone brightly all day. As the coronavirus restrictions were being eased to enable us to come out of a three month period in hibernation, many families and friends went to the parks and beaches to be together again, to relax out-of-doors, and to try and enjoy the start of a little normality.

I decided to walk again through the streets of Edinburgh, the silent city, hoping I might be lucky to get a few more photographs that in years to come might be of interest to — well, whoever. I was not to be disappointed and here I am standing on the roof of Waverley Station, well that's what Waverley Bridge is, built between 1894 and 1896 by 'Blyth and Westland'.

Until the end of March this was one of the busiest streets in the Capital, being quiet only for a few brief hours between around 1 and 5am. At other times it was a hub of vibrant activity for tourists and residents going about their business and pleasure.

They may have been going to, or coming from, the railway station. Lothian Buses has its principal Information Centre at the far end on the left, and the Express 100 bus service to and from Edinburgh Airport operated from here every few minutes twenty-four hours a day. The Bridge has always been a vital link between North and South Edinburgh, where queues of traffic intersperse with thousands of people and cyclists going up and down here all day long. And as if that wasn't enough, there were usually many tour buses starting and ending their journeys nearly every day of the year, squeezing in and out of this narrow corridor.

This though is 2020. Silence, calm, tranquillity — unimaginable words, never before associated with Waverley Bridge on a warm and sunny Saturday afternoon.

It was the end of the 13th week of coronavirus restrictions, and as I made my way up to Princes Street I had one last look back. I wondered if I'd ever see this scene like this again.

INDEX - A to Z